Endor

Spiritual Musings from the Headlines of a Newspaper

In a world increasingly marred by misinformation, confusion, and moral ambiguity, one looks for a beacon of clarity and truth. It is easy to lose sight of our spiritual compass and drift away from the core principles that guide our faith. *Spiritual Musings from the Headlines of a Newspaper* is more than just a response to current events; it is a call to engage with the world around us in a discerning and faithful manner. By integrating biblical principles with everyday experiences, this book equips readers to confront the cultural lies that permeate our society, and stand firm in their convictions with grace and wisdom.

Judy McEachran
Pastor, Author, and Word Weaver President Group 28

In *Spiritual Musings from the Headlines of a Newspaper*, John Rabins offers a thoughtful and bold guide for Christians seeking clarity in a world of confusion. Tackling today's most controversial issues—such as gender identity, abortion, and entitlement mentality—Rabins uses a biblical lens to expose the deceptions that often dominate cultural conversations. Each chapter is insightful, engaging, and filled with practical wisdom for navigating modern challenges while remaining grounded in God's truth. This book is a timely resource for those wanting to stand strong in their faith while ministering with love and grace in a divided world.

Susan Neal
RN, MBA, MHS, Author of *12 Ways to Age Gracefully*

Societal pressure is robbing us of both our right to believe in unpopular stances, and rational analysis of the issues we face. In a fog of media bombardment that shouts at us with unsubstantiated claims, it's becoming unacceptable to think logically, and independently, about the world in which we live. John Rabins breaks through that fog using humor, intentionally ludicrous stories, and thought-provoking comparisons to provide reminders of the logical underpinnings of a biblical worldview. These observations are a breath of fresh air to equip Christians and challenge non-Christians to re-evaluate our world in light of reason, heartfelt concern, and common sense.

Kristen Paris
Health Coach, Founder of *Powered by Health*,
and Author of *Beauty from Ashes*

John Rabins has prepared for us a candid description of today's cultural puzzles and addresses each with truth and encouragement concerning where we need to go as a church. A solid read with common sense answers from a man with a passion to follow Christ.

Carter Bradley Benedict
Pastor, Evangelist, Cowboy Poet, and Singer-Songwriter

Dr. John Rabins has done it again! His first two books, *Defined by Fire* and *Spiritual Musings from the Saddle of a Bicycle*, were biographical and cover life-changing events in John's life. This writing is a personally thoughtful expression of his political views and nails what many of us believe. I heartily endorse it and encourage everyone you know to read it and be moved in your spirit.

Orwyn Sampson
Brigadier General (retired), USAF

Spiritual Musings from the Headlines of a Newspaper

A Biblical Compass for Christians Navigating a Culture of Lies

Jh. Rab — Acts 17:11

JOHN RABINS

Publisher Information

Firewall Press, LLC
firewallpress.com
Colorado Springs, Colorado

For more information or to contact the author, please email john@johnrabins.com.

ISBN 978-1-7345190-4-4 (softcover)
ISBN 978-1-7345190-5-1 (eBook)

Cover design: Terry Dugan
Cover photo credits:
Newsprint: tostphoto@AdobeStock
Bible with Compass: RapidEye@iStock.com
Editorial team: Marcus Costantino, Cristina Wright, and Amy Sinnott
Interior design: eBookBurner Technologies
Publishing services provided by BelieversBookServices.com

First printing: 2024

Printed in the United States of America

Dedication

I proudly dedicate this book to a man who has positively influenced me since I was in high-school—Air Force Brigadier General (retired) Orwyn Sampson, or simply O, as he is affectionately called. A letter I wrote him in 2022 will best serve to lay the background for this choice:

February 6, 2022

Dear O,

Two weeks ago, our men's Bible study teacher challenged us to share about one individual in our lives who had a significant impact on us—a mentor to be precise. Here's how he worded his request:

"None of us has enjoyed success without input from many individuals during our formative years (parents, relatives, teachers, teammates, co-workers, military buddies, or close friends). So, think of one specific mentor who provided you with compassionate thought, time, purpose, experience, or example to light your path and make a dynamic impact on your spirit."

Dear friend, YOU were the one who came to mind, and the one I spoke about: from how you, an Air Force officer, called to invite *me*, a high school student, to visit the Academy; to arranging a commercial helicopter flight from my home to the airport (and duplicating that at the end of the trip) to make it easier on my parents; to your hosting me at your home that weekend, while I got to visit cadets and experience Academy life; to your taking me under your wing—as a student in your human anatomy class and as a member of the Academy gymnastics team. Your mentorship didn't stop there—it impacted my life later when I found myself a member of the faculty, and it continues even to this very day.

But by far the most indelible memory of your mentoring me was during the period I was investigating the Christian faith. My coming from a Jewish background may have made your job more difficult, I think, but you faithfully answered all my questions with great discernment and patience, demonstrating a wonderful example of what it means to be a Christ-follower. I will never forget your telling me once that, even without the promise of Heaven, you'd want to live as a Christian. Wow, that simple comment moved me then, and it still does today.

Thank you, O, for all you've done for me over the years—you're an amazing mentor!

Spiritual Musings from the Headlines of a Newspaper: A Biblical Compass for Christians Navigating a Culture of Lies is written specifically for those who've developed critical thinking skills in viewing the world around them. When I think about all this great man has taught me over the years, *most* important to me was just that—*how to think critically*, a skill so necessary, yet sorely lacking in our culture today!

Honestly, I have *no* explanation for this photo with O at my commissioning ceremony. But one thing I know for sure—his hand of grace, freely given to me over the years, clearly shows up in it!

Contents

Acknowledgements

I'm in debt to the following who've contributed to this work, mostly by their encouragement and sound advice:

1. Jerry White, President Emeritus of the Navigators International, who helped with the original concept and taught me the importance of writing persuasively without antagonizing.

2. Eva Marie Everson, CEO of Word Weavers International, who is an encourager of all encouragers.

3. My Colorado Springs-based and my internet-based Word Weavers groups who've critically reviewed the chapters during development. Their insight has made what I consider a powerful work even more compelling.

4. The Westside Community Center Thursday Bible Study members who've been a terrific cheering section throughout the work's development.

Foreword

*W*hen you read this book by Dr. John Rabins, I'd be surprised if you do not squirm in your chair. It is both provocative and stimulating. It talks about subjects we were taught to avoid if we want to "get along." Even in the church, we hesitate to honestly discuss these vital issues for fear of offending our friends. But I wonder, could our avoidance be offensive to our God? Jesus never avoided uncomfortable topics or the "elephant" in the room—though I see no biblical reference to elephants! He spoke directly to the difficult and divisive issues in the Roman/Jewish community with compassion and yet with powerful clarity. He confronted evil and hypocrisy. Yet He related to, and even loved, sinners. His disciples were mystified, and His enemies were confounded and angered. But He still spoke. Should we not follow His example both in content and spirit? Jesus *was* God, so He wielded true authority. We also wield the authority of the Scriptures. We must speak where it speaks, but also give grace where it does not speak. We should employ scientific and ethical knowledge to fill in the gaps where Scripture is not absolute.

John has chosen these hot-button topics because they flood the newspapers, radio, and other media. They comprise so much of the political dialogue. You will be amused by the "ludicrity" (a new word I have invented) of his opening stories. Yet those stories get our attention to consider the reality of the topic of each chapter. John has said some things you may not agree with. That's perfectly OK—hopefully, it will make you think and investigate further.

"'Come now and let us reason together,' says the Lord" (Isaiah 1:18, NASB). Have we forgotten how to do that?

Have we avoided uncomfortable conversations with other believers? Have we forgotten how to speak truth with love and compassion? Can we remain friends with those who have different views? I learned to do this on scientific and technical issues in my career. But somehow, we find it harder to do among believing friends. And with those who are not believers? Well, this is an excellent resource to engender discussions on each of these topics.

So, approach this book with skepticism and openness. Use it to stimulate your own study and thinking. John did not intend to do an exhaustive exposition on each topic, but rather encourage you to do that. So, the ball is in your court to read, reflect, and come to your own conclusions. These are serious cultural and scriptural issues. We should take them seriously, engaging with prayer, reflection, research, and open discussion with friends.

Jerry White, Ph.D.
International President Emeritus
The Navigators

Introduction: We Get Awfully Worked Up Over—What, Exactly?

*H*ere's some frank self-disclosure: I find myself worked up these days over the state of the world, but more importantly, over the condition of the United States, the country I grew up in with great respect for its principles of freedom, justice, and equal opportunity for all. And this truly means *all*—rich or poor, black or white, male or female—you name it. I believed that even I could grow up to be president of this great country. These God-given rights were important to me, even when I didn't believe in God.

The day I graduated from the United States Air Force Academy, I gained respect for these principles of freedom even more, as I cited the oath of office:

"I (state your full name), having been appointed an officer in the United States Air Force in the grade of Second Lieutenant, do solemnly swear (or affirm) that I will support and defend the Constitution of the United States against all enemies, foreign and domestic, that I will bear true faith and allegiance to the same; that I take this obligation freely, without any mental reservation or purpose of evasion; and that I will well and faithfully discharge the duties of the office on which I am about to enter, so help me God."

And a twenty-five-year Air Force career instilled them deeper yet.

Don't misunderstand me—I still think we live in the greatest country the world has ever known, but I worry about what it is becoming.

In our relatively short history as a country on the world stage, we've been immersed in numerous conflicts with *foreign* enemies. I think of World Wars I and II, the Korean war, the Vietnam conflict, and others. Today, while we yet have foreign enemies that bear monitoring, I see threats coming from *within* our very fabric, like never before, that threaten life as we know it. It reminds me of cancer, a threat from within.

I'm bothered by what I read in the newspapers, what I view on television and social media, and what is imposed upon me in my day-to-day living. I resent the scare tactic that climate change will destroy the earth in just a few years. I hurt deeply when I'm told a baby in a mother's womb is only a piece of tissue, not a human being created in God's image. It also floors me that some who concede the baby may be human see little or no value in that life. My stomach turns as I feel pressured to believe a woman can actually become a man when I *know* that's impossible.

I wonder why a disproportionate number of minorities appear in television commercials recently when I believe they represent a much smaller fraction of our society. And there's plenty more.

The overarching question I wrestle with is, "Are we being pushed to adopt new beliefs that differ fundamentally from historically accepted biblical doctrine? Are we being lured to accept a new definition of *normal?*"

There seems to be a growing sense of hatred, discontent, and fear across the culture, the likes of which I don't remember experiencing as a boy growing up in a suburb near Los Angeles. I remember playing games with kids on our neighborhood streets; there was no need to fear being outside—alone or with others. Sometimes a bunch of us would walk to the local creek to catch tadpoles and frogs. I recall having dinners or playing at neighbors' homes, having them spend time at ours, and even going on vacation with some of them. We felt as though our family extended beyond the walls of our own homes.

It's not that way anymore. People are scared, angry, and far less trusting of others: They're staying home more. They're not gathering as a community. They don't visit their neighbors; in fact, they often don't even *know* their neighbors. People are tired of arguing about abortion rights, division over skin color, gender identity, eco-activism, evolution, and so many more controversial topics.

What's causing all this? Is it the increase in crime, such as auto theft or looting, without any consequences? Is it government-imposed mask mandates during COVID, which robbed us of our identity? Could it be the increased yelling and finger-pointing between the political parties and the media? Is it possible that these are only contributors and not the root cause?

That's what I think—these are simply secondary causes, *all* stemming from a far more fundamental reason. And just what is this reason? I think it stems directly from how God is viewed by our culture. That view has changed dramatically in recent years from one in which God was central to our daily living, to one that was OK with Him, as long as He remained on your side of the fence, and now to one which wants no part of Him.

We must remember that the United States was founded upon biblical principles, *vis-a-vis* the Declaration of Independence, which in its first sentence claims:

> . . . to assume among the powers of the earth, the separate and equal station to which the Laws of Nature and of Nature's God entitle them, . . .

and in its second paragraph:

> We hold these truths to be self-evident, that all men are created equal, that they are endowed by their Creator with certain unalienable Rights, that among these are Life, Liberty, and the pursuit of Happiness.

The Pledge of Allegiance declares us to be "one nation under God." True, the US Constitution never explicitly mentions God or the divine, but the same cannot be said of the nation's state constitutions. In fact, God or the divine is mentioned at least once in each of the fifty state constitutions and nearly 200 times overall. Furthermore, the Liberty Bell is inscribed with Leviticus 25:10: ". . . *and proclaim liberty throughout the land to all its inhabitants.*" We've walked away from that foundation, as did the Israelites of Isaiah's day:

> We all, like sheep, have gone astray,
> each of us has turned to our own way;

and the LORD has laid on Him
the iniquity of us all.
Isaiah 53:6

Now, doesn't this passage from Isaiah only reinforce what we see with our own eyes? And today, aren't we suffering the consequences of our wandering from His plan? The "Him" mentioned in the verse above is none other than our Messiah, Jesus Christ. His sacrifice on the cross paid the price for all of our sins—past, present, and future. Although we continue to sin while in our earthly bodies, He never intended for any of us to flaunt our sins and then claim hate when Christians express disdain for the sins. I'm thinking of events such as Pride Month, for example. Pride in what, exactly? Seems to me it's pride in behavior the Bible categorically condemns. Isn't it interesting that what used to be encouraged as healthy disagreement in discussion is now labeled hate speech?

Spiritual Musings from the Headlines of a Newspaper is for Christians who need better strategies for combatting the lies of the enemy (Satan) that divide us as human beings. Basically, it offers an understanding of who God is and what He says about things that matter at the heart of people. You don't have to agree on a surface level with everything (or anything) I suggest. What I ask is that you carefully consider the content in the light and instruction of Scripture, allowing God to speak to you.

Each chapter begins with a story that may, admittedly, seem ludicrous (even unbelievable) but is intended to be useful in convincing those caught up in these lies that they are believing the very same lie about themselves or their worldview. Each is intentionally short to enhance memorability when help is needed in conversation. Each chapter ends with a heartfelt prayer, recognizing that, not only does God hear our prayers, but He is often moved to change things. The common thread in each piece is the question, "Who is God to you?" Is it the One who created the universe and everything in it, including *you*, who thus has the sovereign right to decide everything He chooses to, or—is it *you*?

The very first chapter of the Bible categorically answers this question: "So God created mankind in *His* own image, in the image of God He created them . . ." (Genesis 1:27a). So, why do so many today create God in *their* own image? *That* is the question of the hour.

Before we can answer that question, we must take a look at Satan, the source of so many lies. He's also called the enemy, devil, adversary, tempter, serpent, evil one, murderer, father of lies, and more. Scripture makes it plain that he is, in fact, a liar and is used as a tool to confuse, discourage, and destroy both Christians and non-Christians alike, as seen in the Old Testament: "'. . . it is I who have created the destroyer to wreak havoc . . .'" (Isaiah 54:16b), and the New Testament: "Be alert and of sober mind. Your enemy the devil prowls around like a roaring lion looking for someone to devour" (1 Peter 5:8).

Satan tempts us to sin, causing us to doubt our salvation and thwart our witness. He blinds the eyes of many and masquerades as an angel of light (2 Corinthians 11:14). He plays plenty more roles, but the Scriptures are clear that he is no friend of ours, and he's effective at his job. He's particularly versed in telling half-truths to mislead, as we observe in his encounter with Eve in the Garden of Eden:

> Now the serpent was more crafty than any of the wild animals the Lord God had made. He said to the woman, "Did God really say, 'You must not eat from any tree in the garden?'" The woman said to the serpent, "We may eat fruit from the trees in the garden, but God did say, 'You must not eat fruit from the tree that is in the middle of the garden, and you must not touch it, or you will die.'"

"You will not certainly die," the serpent said to the woman. "For God knows that when you eat from it your eyes will be opened, and you will be like God, knowing good and evil." When the woman saw that the fruit of the tree was good for food and pleasing to the eye, and also desirable for gaining wisdom, she took some and ate it. She also gave some to her husband, who was with her, and he ate it. Then the eyes of both of them were opened, and they realized they were naked; so they sewed fig leaves together and made coverings for themselves.
Genesis 3:1-7

So, we see he's been busily at work from the beginning, and he appears to be ramping up his efforts today. What's interesting to me is that his most effective tool is convincing Christians that he, in fact, *doesn't* exist. But Jesus mentions him numerous times in the New Testament, leaving no doubt that *He* views him as real:

Jesus turned and said to Peter, "Get behind me, Satan! You are a stumbling block to me; you do not have in mind the concerns of God, but merely human concerns."
Matthew 16:23 [also recounted in Mark 8:33]

Then Jesus was led by the Spirit into the wilderness to be tempted by the devil. After fasting forty days and forty nights, he was hungry. The tempter came to him and said, "If you are the Son of God, tell these stones to become bread."

Jesus answered, "It is written: 'Man shall not live on bread alone, but on every word that comes from the mouth of God.'"

Then the devil took him to the holy city and had him stand on the highest point of the temple. "If you are the Son of God," he said, "throw yourself down. For it is written:

'He will command his angels concerning you, and they will lift you up in their hands, so that you will not strike your foot against a stone.'"

Jesus answered him, "It is also written: 'Do not put the Lord your God to the test.'"

Again, the devil took him to a very high mountain and showed him all the kingdoms of the world and their splendor. "All this I will give you," he said, "if you will bow down and worship me."

Jesus said to him, "Away from me, Satan! For it is written: 'Worship the Lord your God, and serve him only.'"

Then the devil left him, and angels came and attended him.
Matthew 4:1-11

"You belong to your father, the devil, and you want to carry out your father's desires. He was a murderer from the beginning, not holding to the truth, for there is no truth in him. When he lies, he speaks his native language, for he is a liar and the father of lies."
John 8:44 [Jesus addressing the Pharisees]

Not only did Jesus view Satan as a real enemy, but so did the Old and New Testament writers, calling him by one of his names at least eighty times. In fact, he's referred to thirty-eight times in thirty-six verses in the New Testament. Of course, while this knowledge of our having a real enemy can be depressing, we need not fear, as there's exceptionally good news:

> You, dear children, are from God and have overcome
> . . . because the One who is in you [the Lord] is
> greater than the one who is in the world [Satan].
> 1 John 4:4

> "I have told you these things, so that in me you may
> have peace. In this world you will have trouble. But
> take heart! I have overcome the world."
> John 16:33

We also know that God at times can use Satan as a tool to strengthen and build up His saints:

> Consider it pure joy, my brothers, whenever you
> face trials of many kinds, because you know that
> the testing of your faith develops perseverance.
> Perseverance must finish its work so that you may
> be mature and complete, not lacking anything.
> James 1:2-4

Something I once wrote in my Bible margin next to the passage above blesses me each time I read James; it was spoken by someone in my church:

> "I don't know why Satan doesn't just give up and
> go away because everything he brings into our lives
> God uses to strengthen us!"

So now, back to the question of the hour: Why do so many today create God in *their* image? Can there be any doubt that it's Satan, the enemy of our souls? Recall that his primary goal is to keep us from believing God.

I vividly recall chastising our younger son, Nate, years ago when he was misbehaving in the kitchen—he was only two years old at the time. I do not remember the infraction, but I'll never forget his reaction. He defiantly placed his hands on his hips and loudly declared, "I do what I want!" We tried hard not to laugh but couldn't contain ourselves—it was so cute. But doesn't this highlight the central theme running through this book? Are we subject to authority outside of ourselves, or not? Is God real, or is He just someone we've conjured up in our minds?

When I was growing up, the word *woke* simply meant arousal from sleep. But the word woke is bantered about frequently these days and has an entirely different meaning. One original, narrow definition derived from the African-America Vernacular (AAVE) is "to be alert to racial prejudice and discrimination."[1] But it's broadened some since 2010 to encompass a wider awareness of social inequalities such as sexism, identity politics (based on a particular identity, such as race, nationality, religion, gender, sexual orientation, social background, caste, and social class), and social justice.[2]

In my opinion, the hot-button issues discussed in this book have divided us as a culture and beg the following questions: Are woke ideology and these issues related in any way? Might individualism and secular humanism serve as the breeding ground for woke ideology? How do communism and socialism play into what's going on in our culture today?

I'm troubled at the increasing attacks against conservative Christianity and feel as though *wokeism* is putting us all to *sleep*, meaning Christians are experiencing societal pressure to accept as true, or at least tolerate, that which the Scriptures adamantly oppose. We're being lured to compromise our values and accept as "normal" that which simply is not. As Christ followers, we must defend the clear teaching of the Scriptures, even—especially—in the face of opposition. We

---

[1] Clea Calcutt, "French education minister's anti-woke mission," October 19, 2021, *Politico*, October 19, 2021.
[2] www.merriam-webster.com/dictionary/woke.

must not buckle to societal pressures under the guise of getting along:

> You adulterous people! Do you not know that friendship with the world is enmity with God? Therefore whoever wishes to be a friend of the world makes himself an enemy of God. Or do you suppose it is to no purpose that the Scripture says, "He yearns jealously over the spirit that He has made to dwell in us"? But He gives more grace. Therefore it says, "God opposes the proud but gives grace to the humble." Submit yourselves therefore to God. Resist the devil, and he will flee from you. Draw near to God, and He will draw near to you. Cleanse your hands, you sinners, and purify your hearts, you double-minded. Be wretched and mourn and weep. Let your laughter be turned to mourning and your joy to gloom. Humble yourselves before the Lord, and He will exalt you.
> James 4:4-10

And we must remember to do so with the loving attitude of Christ. Thus, I've been intentionally mindful as I've written of something Jerry White, President Emeritus of The Navigators, International, shared with me: "One cannot persuade and antagonize at the same time." We must be mindful of the fact that loving God and loving our neighbor go together. Defending the name of God and His will on earth can and should be done in loving relationships with humility.

Do you, reader, feel like I do sometimes—frustrated, depressed, and hopeless by what we observe in our culture? Do you at times feel as though it's just not worth it, that some people are simply unreachable? May we never forget our God never gives up on us and can reach the *unreachable*, e.g., the apostle Paul, to name just one of many extraordinary examples. Would you like to be better at winning arguments? How about defending God or Christianity? Are you one who wants to "save America?" Would you like to follow Jesus more closely so your prodigal(s) will come home? Or, perhaps, you simply want to learn to love in truth. Whatever your goal(s), this book is for you. If you learn to use these strategies, by the power of the Holy Spirit, under the authority of Jesus, to the glory of the Father, and out of love for your neighbor, you will be better positioned to fulfill the Great Commission:

> ". . . go and make disciples of all nations, baptizing them in the name of the Father and of the Son and of the Holy Spirit, and teaching them to obey everything I have commanded you. And surely I will be with you always, to the very end of the age." Matthew 28:19-20

I'm heartened that our God is faithful and will see us through all of this as He has in the past—He *is* in control, after all. Please don't misunderstand me—I love this country and the Godly principles on which it was founded; we just have some work to do, as it's well worth defending. May you find these chapters useful *and persuasive* as you minister with love and grace to those caught up in these lies.

Is it OK to Arbitrarily Abort Unborn Puppies?

The Sanctity of Human Life

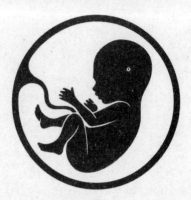

*A*boy found a chubby dog on his way home from school and brought it home with him, hoping his mom would let him keep her. His mom saw the dog was about to deliver puppies and told him they couldn't keep that many dogs as theirs was a small house, suitable for only one pet, perhaps two at most. The boy felt very sad, as he'd been asking his mom for a pet dog for quite some time.

Even in such a short time, he had developed an attachment to the dog and felt desperate to keep her, so he took her to a park nearby and fed her poison, causing her to miscarry the litter; he then returned home with a dog that was no longer pregnant. His mom relented and allowed him to keep her.

***

I find this simple story to be disturbing for several reasons. First, the boy's decision was selfish without regard for any value of the puppies the female dog was carrying. Second, since he figured he owned the new dog, he owned the puppies as well and could do with them as he wished, even if it meant their destruction. And third, I'm bothered by his mom's callousness at his behavior. Perhaps most concerning to me, however, is the impact on the boy's character as he cemented both the tendency to take the easy way out and the idea that he had the right to eliminate inconveniences, even at the cost of another's life.

This, perhaps, is the most difficult topic for me to write about for several reasons, not the least of which is that it is such a hotly-contested issue. One cannot listen to the radio, watch TV, follow political news, or even go out in public these days without hearing or seeing a myriad of opinions on the topic. If you're like me, it can be most discouraging, regardless of the side of the aisle you are on. Undoubtedly, it is one of the most critical issues we must deal with in today's world, and the main reason I chose to start this book off with it.

With all of this in mind, let's examine three lies the enemy has foisted on women facing abortion:

Lie #1. A baby in the womb is nothing more than a piece of tissue, and, consequently, just part of the woman's body for which she alone has control.

Lie #2. Babies in the womb, while human beings, are not valuable in certain circumstances, and thus can be discarded to avoid a "bad life."

Lie #3. Babies in the womb are *whatever* the mother wishes to call them.

We'll now place each one of these under the light to help understand why they are indeed lies.

1. A baby in the womb is nothing more than a piece of tissue, and, consequently, just part of the woman's body for which she alone has control.

God Says Otherwise

When does life begin? Conception? Heartbeat detected? Birth? Breathing on its own? Is it just me, or does this seem rather arbitrary? God doesn't mince words as He describes, through David's writing, the beginning of life:

> For you created my inmost being; you knit me together *in my mother's womb*. I praise you because I am fearfully and wonderfully made; your works are wonderful, I know that full well. My frame was not hidden from you when I was made in the secret place. All the days ordained for me were written in your book before one of them came to be.
> Psalm 139:13-16

> When Elizabeth heard Mary's greeting, the baby *leaped in her womb*, and Elizabeth was filled with the Holy Spirit. In a loud voice she exclaimed... As soon as the sound of your greeting reached my ears, *the baby in my womb leaped for joy.*
> Luke 1:41-42, 44

We learn from the Bible that God creates human beings *inside* the womb. He is in control of the process from the very beginning. He is the One who creates life by knitting us together. Yes, pregnancy typically involves a man and a woman, but it also involves the Holy Spirit. As such, we don't get the final say on when life begins or at what point life has value. God does. And He says all of humanity matters the moment He conceived of us in His mind and gave us life in our mother's womb.

I find it fascinating that just twenty-four to forty-eight hours after fertilization, per a digital article in *Live Action*,[3] "pregnancy can be confirmed by detecting a hormone called 'early pregnancy factor,' or EPF, in the mother's blood. This substance helps prevent the mother's immune system from rejecting the soon-to-be implanted embryo and allows pregnancy to proceed." In other words, well before a baby implants into the lining of his/her mother's womb, which occurs around day six, he/she is already sending out signals that he/she is alive and is not some foreign substance to be rejected by the mother's immune system.

Let's examine what else occurs in the first few weeks following fertilization:

Week 1: The embryo attaches to the uterine wall, and the placenta begins to form.

Week 2: Early on in the first trimester, the baby's brain is the first organ to appear, with its three main divisions, and the forming heart can be seen.

Week 3: The blood and blood vessels appear. The heart begins to beat between days sixteen and twenty-one.

Weeks 4 and 5: Eyes, lungs, and the cerebral hemispheres of the brain appear and begin growing quickly. Kidneys form.

Weeks 6 and 7: Brain waves begin, and hands, feet, and legs appear and begin to move. The heart now has four chambers, and the baby can rotate his/her head and have hiccups. Ovaries (for girls) and testes (for boys) form.[4]

---

[3] https://www.liveaction.org/news/first-trimester-babies-complex/?gad_source=1&gclid=Cj0KCQjwn9y1BhC2ARIsAG5IY-7YXbwNB6xsBNyVEtfX08GkH0mrt7DnuDT67uomYVDH4J2E5bMbxMEaArBxEALw_wcB.

[4] Ibid

And it goes on from there. My point is that it actually resembles a human *baby* from conception, not just a mass of tissue.

2. Babies in the womb, while human beings, are not valuable in certain circumstances, and thus can be discarded to avoid a "bad life."

Who Are We to Decide?

Is attempting to keep a baby from a "bad life" sensible in any way? Truly, who are *we* to decide that? A few illustrative examples come to mind:

1. Stephen Hawking
    Being diagnosed early in life with ALS forced him to use a full-time powered chair and speak with the assistance of a computer in later years. Despite these disabilities, he became one of the most well-known physicists in the world, respected for his thoughts on the universe, principally in the areas of general relativity and quantum mechanics. His best-selling book *A Brief History of Time* remained on the New York Times bestseller list for more than four and a half years!

2. Helen Keller
    Completely deaf and blind by the age of nineteen months, here is an author, political activist, and lecturer who was portrayed in the movie *The Miracle Worker*. In it, her teacher Ann Sullivan developed a language she was able to understand. Helen was the first deaf and blind person to earn a Bachelor of Arts degree. She went on to write and publish twelve books.

3. Stevie Wonder
   Born blind due to Retinopathy of Prematurity (ROP), Stevie went on to become one of the most storied and successful singer-songwriters. He recorded over thirty top-ten singles.

4. Michael Wagner
   Unknown to the world, and not famous by any stretch of the imagination, he is one of my all-time favorite optometry patients. Michael had Down Syndrome but never let it keep him from creating laughter and joy wherever he went; I always looked forward to his yearly visits. Having a huge passion for sports, he'd participated from age four in swimming, skiing, bowling, and basketball. He could tell you anything you wanted to know about his favorite team, the Denver Broncos, always sporting a Broncos hat and jersey. He held jobs in the food industry until his cognitive decline in 2020. He passed away in 2021 at the age of sixty-one. You might call his life a pretty ordinary one, but Michael touched me, and others, in ways no one else could.

This is but a small handful of the many successful lives of people who struggled with great disability. I could go on with more stories just like these, but hopefully, my point is clear: Imagine if Stephen's, or Helen's, or Stevie's, or Michael's mother (or father) learned of their disability before birth, in time to *do something about it*. Wouldn't our world have missed something *very* special? In light of these accounts, perhaps Jesus' words in the Gospel of John should take on additional importance:

The thief comes only to steal and kill and destroy;
I have come that they may have life, and have it to
the full.
John 10:10

3. Babies in the womb are whatever the mother wishes to call them.

This is likely the most dangerous lie of all. No human, not even an unwilling mother, can step into God's shoes. The question that must be asked is, "Is there such a thing as absolute truth?" To answer that, let's look at the expressions "my truth" and "your truth" so commonly used these days. People use these to convince others of something using only anecdotal evidence. They are sincere in their beliefs, but it's possible to be sincerely wrong. How can one person announce her truth that one plus one equals two, while another says his truth is that it's four, and they *both* be right? The fact is that our personal experiences don't change the nature of truth. Our opinions can be different, but the truth doesn't change just because we have different experiences. Truly, if we think about it long enough, we *all* believe in absolute truth, so long as it agrees with "our" truth.

Let's see what the Bible, which claims itself to *be perfect and absolute truth*, says:

> The law of the LORD is perfect, converting the soul: the testimony of the LORD is sure, making wise the simple.
> Psalm 19:7

> Your righteousness is everlasting and Your law is true.
> Psalm 119:142

In other words, the Bible claims to be without error, and, thus (if it is), can and should be trusted. These, and other Scriptures like them, are either right (and to be believed) or wrong (and can be ignored).

Before concluding this chapter, let's look at some interesting nuances about the topic:

Abortion laws speak about the word *viability*. What does the word mean, anyway? According to most modern thinking, a viable pregnancy is one in which the baby can be born and have a reasonable chance of survival. By contrast, a nonviable pregnancy is one in which the baby has no chance of being born alive. If we think about it for any length of time, babies after their birth are *totally* dependent on mom (or another human), just as they are before they are born, and truly are no more viable than before birth. Oh, but they're able to breathe on their own, some might say. What does breathing have to do with viability? Are they any less dependent on an adult just because they can breathe? If you doubt that, ask yourself what would happen if a breathing baby were left alone for three days. What about babies after their birth (or even teens or adults) who cannot breathe without the aid of a ventilator? Is that some special exception? The inconsistencies in arguments are indeed puzzling!

How did the expression, "women's healthcare," replace the word *abortion*? Is this nothing more than a euphemism for a far more polarizing word? And speaking of euphemisms, why do we use the dehumanizing word *fetus*, instead of *unborn child*, when the word itself comes from the Latin and literally means "little one" or "offspring"?

Some argue that abortion should be available in the event of rape, as a specific example. A challenging issue, to be sure, but should such a horrific event, as awful as it is, minimize the value of the human life she's carrying? And as sensitive as this issue is, we have to ask if the baby must be sentenced to death to pay for the sin of the (rapist) father. While these sensitive topics are difficult, they certainly bear discussion.

In sum, the bottom line for me is the question, "Who's in charge, anyway? Is it *us*, or is it *God*?" Excluding the sensitive case of rape for the moment, does a woman really have the right to "choose" at *any* time, or does that right end "in the bedroom" (at the point of conception)? I'm certainly aware of the difficult nature of this question, but again—might the words abortion, fetus, women's choice, or women's healthcare be euphemized excuses for our choice not to follow God's laws in most cases of unwanted pregnancy? And we have already established that the Word of God shows His laws are for our good, never to harm us. His love for us exceeds our wildest imagination, and the longer it takes us to appreciate how much He cares for us, the more foolish we are, as the psalmist David so concisely wrote:

> The *fool* says in his heart, "There is no God."
> Psalm 14:1 [repeated in Psalm 53:1]

Why do you suppose it bothers so many people to think about God loving and nurturing us at our conception?

My Prayer: Lord, help me to see the value in human life as You do from the moment of conception. May I not be deceived into believing extraneous circumstances can *ever* change that. May I never replace Your sovereignty with my own. Help me see with Your tender, loving eyes the fear and *desperation* attending pregnant mothers without the means to care for the beautiful lives growing within them. May I be a part of the provision they need to face the overwhelming choice to follow You instead of society's easy outs.

Seriously, Is That a Real Maserati?

Gender Identity

*T*here was a man who loved his old car, a 1963 Mercury Comet, so much that he had it restored and painted at an auto body shop. All the dents were removed, the body was perfectly sanded/smoothed, and it was painted a bright racy red. It cost him a lot of money, and the finished product was positively beautiful. The owner was quite pleased with the resulting look (and himself). Then he placed a Maserati hood ornament on the front of the car and offered it for sale as a genuine 2018 Maserati for $35,000.

Seventeen people responded to the ad and came to look at the car. The first sixteen said the car looked amazing but was not, in fact, a Maserati. The owner became angry, accusing each one of hatred by disrespecting *his* determination that the car was, in fact, an authentic Maserati. The seventeenth bought the lie, *and the car*, haggling the price down to a mere $31,500. He patted himself on the back as he drove away for his amazing negotiation skills.

***

When I was growing up in the 50s and 60s, there were boys and there were girls. Admittedly, some rare outliers were confused about how they fit into society, but most accepted exactly who God made them to be. Why? Because we learned the truth in biology class that there are differences between men and women—a man has a penis and an XY set of chromosomes, while a woman has a vagina and an XX set of chromosomes.

Our current culture is confusing to me. Today, no one seems to know the difference between a man and a woman, *vis-a-vis* a liberal Supreme Court nominee during her recent confirmation hearing who, on being asked what a woman is, responded, "I don't know."

With increasing numbers, men are deciding they're really women, and boys are deciding they're really girls. And it's the same thing for women/girls who view themselves as men/boys. Sadly, our culture increasingly endorses such decisions as *normal*, and people are *encouraged* to undergo gender-disfiguring/life-altering surgeries to match their appearance with their gender-view of themselves. Those hurt the most, in my opinion, are the boys and girls going through the conflicting thoughts that are considered *quite normal* in experiencing puberty.

It used to be believed generally that there was one God and two genders. Now, the world believes in many gods and many genders—I've heard as many as fifty-eight—and that number seems to grow by the day! However, God makes no mistakes and knows us better than we know ourselves. He made us in His image and desires that we conform to that image. Truly, our lives are so much more manageable (and wonderful) when we agree with Him.

Back to my youth for a moment—I was taught that in America one could be anything he wanted to be. That sentiment helped foster the idea that we live in the greatest country in the world. While that's still a great thought, it's only in more recent years that I've come to understand we simply *cannot* be that which we cannot be. Everyone *knows* that a Timex watch cannot become a Rolex, a Baldwin piano cannot become a Steinway, and a Mercury Comet can *never* become a Maserati—why is it we believe a man can become a woman?

Should it concern anyone that a male swimmer who competes poorly against other men does so much better against women after "transitioning" into one? I'm thinking of Lia Thomas who, after performing as an average male swimmer *before* "transitioning," won the women's 2022 NCAA's Division 1 500-yard freestyle title *after* doing so. I'm thinking also of the 2020 Tokyo Olympics in which a forty-three-year-old man, Laurel Hubbard, qualified to compete in women's weightlifting after beating a twenty-one-year-old woman who had trained much of her life for that opportunity. It didn't matter that he could not compete with other men; he simply enjoyed a natural and biological edge over the younger women.

What about a "woman" who easily rolls through the Olympic competition to the gold medal, despite previous International Boxing Association (IBA) tests revealing the presence of Y chromosomes in "her" blood? Now, I'm aware of the claims of some that "she" may have a *rare* disorder of sexual development called Developmental Sex Difference (DSD), where high testosterone levels and Y chromosomes may appear within a female body. But that's the exception, not the rule; let's not be distracted from the primary and most common situation—biological males identifying and competing against biological females. It just doesn't work and is simply unfair to women. And why do you suppose we don't see many (if any) female-to-male transgenders seeking to compete at the men's level in sports? Just asking.

Finally, here's something worth considering—data indicates that 82% of transgender individuals have considered killing themselves and 40% have attempted suicide, with suicidality highest among transgender youth.[5] Hmm, I wonder—why should we find that surprising?

The story of creation is found at the very beginning of the first book of the Bible—Genesis. Despite lots of current thoughts on exactly how it happened (see Chapter 4 on Evolution), I prefer to believe the simple account seen in the book of Genesis. God was *there* at the beginning, orchestrating things as He saw fit. None of us, even our most brilliant scientists, can say *they* were. Shouldn't that mean something to us?

> So God created mankind in His own image, in the image of God He created them; *male and female He created them.*
> Genesis 1:27

---

[5] Ashley Austin, Shelley L Craig, Sandra D'Souza, Lauren B McInroy "Suicidality Among Transgender Youth: Elucidating the Role of Interpersonal Risk Factors," *Epub*, April 29, 2020, https://pubmed.ncbi.nlm.nih.gov/32345113/.

Haven't you read, He replied, that at the beginning
the Creator made them male and female . . .
Matthew 19:4

In Matthew's passage, the He who is speaking is none
other than Jesus, who was present at the creation, as well.

Restrooms at Aloha Stadium on Oahu. Can you guess
what went through my mind when I first saw these years
ago? It's interesting that these have since been painted over.

My Prayer: Lord, help me remember that You created me
in Your image! You called me by name for Your purposes.
Help me not only accept who You called me to be but relish
the opportunity to live for You, according to *Your* will. May
I be grateful to live in a country that affords its citizens great
opportunities, but may I never be duped into believing I can
be something that I simply *cannot* be!

Can One Judge an Apple by Its Color?

Skin Color

A man loved apples—not just any apples, *only* red ones; he said his family hated green apples because they tasted bad. He tried one once; his grandmother was making a pie and he sneaked a bite. He was convinced.

But there isn't only one type of green apple; the Granny Smith tastes sour but makes an excellent pie. The Golden Delicious tastes wonderful but is not used in pies. Alternatively, there are sweet red apples and sour ones. Of course, some are just *bad* apples (pun intended).

Apparently, we cannot tell much, if anything, about an apple merely by the color of its skin. All apples look pretty much the same after their peels are removed; thus, the quality of an apple is discovered by its *taste*, what's inside, not its outward appearance.

***

It's the same with people. If you remove the skin from two comparably-sized cadavers, one with dark skin and the other with light, it's difficult to tell them apart. The axiom, you cannot judge a book by its cover, holds true. Yet, isn't that what we do when it comes to skin color?

As I was growing up, I learned the *only* difference in people with different skin colors was the amount of melanin in their skin. I still believe that. But today one cannot watch TV, peruse social media, or read the newspaper without recognizing not everyone feels the same way. And, as in the story about apples above, some unfounded prejudices propagate in families for generations.

The escalating divide over skin color amazes and offends me. What happened to the sentiment in the song, "Jesus Loves the Little Children?"—"Red and yellow, black and white; they are precious in His sight?" And what about Martin Luther King, Jr.'s 1963 dream, "that my four little children will one day . . . not be judged by the color of their skin but by the content of their character?"

In the 60 years since Dr. King's speech, where have we come as a culture? I'm embarrassed to say the racial divide seems to have worsened, although I'm not sure whether it's more of the same, or something else altogether. Could it be that the very *face* of racial division has changed *color*? Has *equal opportunity*, guaranteed by the US Constitution, been replaced by *equal outcome*, which has *never* done anything but polarize? Expecting equal outcomes is antithetical to what distinguishes our nation from so many others, and engenders an entitlement mentality rather than a desire to work hard for what one gets. True equal opportunity should encourage accomplishment and rising above the present to create a better future. What I see today does not appear to encourage anyone, regardless of race or skin color, to become better or to make the world a better place. It feels as though today's culture is fueled by anger and resentment, rather than love, compassion, and understanding. Ask yourself, does *fury* pave the way for tenderness, respect, and cooperation?

I've had many friends of various skin colors over the years, including very dark-skinned individuals with whom my relationships went deep. As I recall, I *never* thought about the differences in our skin colors. But I do today, wondering why I'm more sensitive than ever before. One cannot watch TV commercials today without viewing a highly skewed cross-section of our culture. Might a foreigner watching these commercials logically conclude that America consists of more than 50% Blacks and Browns, 20% Asians, and the rest Caucasians?[6]

My last Air Force assignment was as military director of a research laboratory in Boston. One day, I received an email asking me to nominate my top black scientists for a distinguished award. Three of my black scientists promptly

---

[6] This is my conservative estimate after keeping tally for a week of primetime television viewing. Online research shows percentages for blacks/browns ranging between 33% and 70%.

came into my office at the same time, demanding that I *not* nominate them for such an award, stating that if they cannot compete on their own merits, they wanted no part of it. I got it then, and I get it now. Each of these scientists had a history of great work accomplishments. Their merit lay in their scientific excellence, not in what they looked like. They rightly felt patronized, wanting recognition solely for the right reasons.

I've always wondered why anyone would think racial-centric groups, e.g., the NAACP or the Hispanic Chamber of Commerce, could do anything but divide. I've asked—would it be politically OK to have a NAAWP or a White History Month? How about a Miss White America? The answer is clearly *no* and confusing as eight black women have won the Miss America Pageant since 1983. Would it not be more of a bonding experience if we focused less on skin color and more on personal character? In a nutshell, one should not expect to heal racial discrimination with racial discrimination.

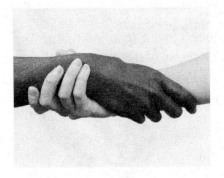

Know that I'm *not* criticizing cultural events, such as Cinco de Mayo celebrations, or Pow Wows. America is not just a melting pot but also a veritable stew, whose distinct parts imbue a unique flavor upon the whole. Recognizing the variety of spices that season our culture simply opens our eyes to the unique contributions of each segment of American heritage. In that sense, differences are to be celebrated and, in celebration, we can truly become a *United* States.

God loves *all* His children, and skin color is irrelevant to their relationship with Him; it's simply a reminder of how much variety our Father has incorporated into His creation. The value He sees in humanity lies deep within our hearts. We must learn to see people His way. Martin Luther King, Jr. did that; isn't it time for us to do the same?

I love this quote by perhaps the most important leader of the movement for African-American civil rights in the nineteenth century, Frederick Douglass:

> "Neither law, learning, nor religion, is addressed to any man's color or race. Science, education, the Word of God, and all the virtues known among men, are recommended to us, not as races, but as men. We are not recommended to love or hate any particular variety of the human family more than any other. Not as Ethiopians; not as Caucasians; not as Mongolians; not as Afro-Americans, or Anglo-Americans, are we addressed, but as men. God and nature speak to our manhood, and to our manhood alone. Here all ideas of duty and moral obligation are predicated."[7]

---

[7] Frederick Douglass, "Blessings of Liberty and Education," *Teaching American History*, September 3, 1894, https://teachingamericanhistory. org/document/blessings-of-liberty-and-education/.

A former American slave and abolitionist in the 1800s, Douglass was well-versed in the Scriptures, particularly those dealing with how God views His children, as the verse in 1 Samuel below points out:

". . . People look at the outward appearance, but the LORD looks at the heart."
1 Samuel 16:7

My Prayer: Lord, help us see Your children as You do. May we be less interested in a person's outward appearance, and more interested in the heart that lies within. Impart to us the understanding that there is only *one* race—the human race. Help us not be as shallow as a man's (or woman's) skin.

C'mon, Did That Sandcastle Appear All by Itself?

Evolution

*T*here was a boy who was fortunate to live at the beach. Each day, when he wasn't in school, he'd wander along the shore, watching other boys and girls making sandcastles. Some of the castles were small and crude while others were large and detailed. But none of them were anything close to what he dreamed about.

As he had a vivid imagination, he figured the wind and waves consistently working on the sand could make an even more magnificent sandcastle, given enough time. So, he staked out an area behind his house and checked every morning to see if a sandcastle had appeared. He did this every day for weeks, then months, then years. To his chagrin, a sandcastle never appeared, not even a crude one, and he was sorely disappointed.

Charles Darwin

***

Isn't that the conventional thinking about evolution, that, given enough time, not only is *anything* possible but even *probable*? This is not unlike the familiar story about giving a monkey enough time to bang on a typewriter at random and expecting the complete works of Shakespeare to eventually appear. My common sense and experience have trouble with that idea. When I was in elementary school, the age of the universe was estimated to be between 1.6 and 2.4 billion years (funny how I recall those exact numbers), and that number has grown tremendously since. Why, you might ask? Because only within highly exaggerated time frames does the *impossible* become *possible*. Intuitively, however, we know that's not right.

Evolution requires order to emerge from disorder—pattern out of chaos. Doesn't that go against our experience? A new car breaks down over time. Furniture wears out. We get slower and less spry as we age. Our experience is supported by the Second Law of Thermodynamics—in a closed system, entropy (a word for disorder) increases. And that's exactly what we see experientially—everything breaks down.

I used to believe in evolution, not because it made sense to me, but because everyone seemed to believe in it. I even had a professor in a college advanced-placement biology class assert on day one that she would be teaching the "fact" of evolution, not the "theory," insisting it was a proven fact. I took her word for it. Over time, after earning a Ph.D. in lasers/optical physics, and becoming a follower of Christ, I began to question why I believed in evolutionary principles as I had. I started asking questions, such as:

1. Doesn't the fact that we observe volcanoes and earthquakes speak of a *young* earth with a hot molten center? Wouldn't an old earth have reached equilibrium by now?
2. If Darwin's "survival of the fittest" was correct, why do we still see cockroaches managing to do so well? Why didn't they sense the need to change?
3. In the fossil record, why do we, at times, find·more complex life forms physically *below* the more elementary ones? Might this perhaps support evolutionary thinking less and a global flood more?
4. Why are we still looking for the missing link between apes and man? Could it be that it doesn't exist and is simply *missing*?
5. If God truly created, as opposed to natural selection, what can we possibly know about the creation except that which He chooses to reveal to us? Aren't we being

presumptuous to think we (or science) can explain it?

Becoming a Christian not only turned my worldview upside down, but it logically answered these questions. Finally, everything made sense!

Let's think about this for a moment.

What do we *know*, with certainty, when we look at a watch? If we're being honest, we know that it was created. Same with a camera.

It should be obvious that someone *designed* and *made* them. Yet, evolution teaches that, over a long enough amount of time (and that's the key), the watch and camera can just appear by accident. Here's what is even more remarkable to me: it teaches that *life* can emerge the same way.

As an optometrist, I *know* the human eye is far more amazing and complex than the most advanced camera; yet evolution teaches that not just the camera, but the eye, and even human life, materialized over a lengthy period. Wow! If, deep down, we *know* a sandcastle cannot form by accident, aren't we demonstrating a bigger leap of faith by thinking a watch, camera, eye, or life itself *can*?

Instead of stretching our imaginations in such an egregious way, wouldn't it be simpler, and more logical, to believe the clear teaching of the Scripture in the Old Testament? Why must we try so hard to figure it out when, if God really created as He said, that may well be impossible? Perhaps we should trust Him, knowing it will all make sense over time.

> In the beginning God created the heavens and the earth.
> Genesis 1:1

> Where were you when I laid the earth's foundation?
> Tell me if you understand.
> Job 38:4

> The fear of the Lord is the beginning of wisdom.
> Proverbs 9:10

My Prayer: Lord, please remind me in everything I see that You created it all *exactly* as You declared in Your Word. Give me a renewed appreciation for the creation account I find in Genesis. May I remain on the narrow pathway, not distracted by those who claim science can explain that which only You can.

I Love the Home My Husband Built for Me So Much, I Wonder—Can I Dump Him?

Eco and Animal Activism

A young man and woman fell in love and got married. At their wedding, they vowed to love, cherish, and protect each other until death would part them. The husband, a very talented real estate developer, built a beautiful home for them to live in. Then, he fully furnished it, including every amenity to make their lives comfortable together. The husband wanted the best for his wife, loving her with his whole heart. He asked her only that she keep their home clean and orderly while he was at work.

She loved her home and began obsessing over it. She placed restrictions on her husband as to what he could or could not do in their home. She became distant from her husband, even preferring to be at home without him rather than with him. She decided she didn't love or need him anymore and eventually filed for divorce. She had forsaken her first love.

***

In like fashion, God made the earth and everything in it for our use. His creation was beautiful and perfect, and His charge was for Adam and Eve to tend and care for it, instructing them, "Be fruitful and increase in number; fill the earth and subdue it. Rule over the fish in the sea and the birds in the sky and over every living creature that moves on the ground" (Genesis 1:28). He gave them only one rule—not to eat from the tree of knowledge of good and evil in the middle of the Garden of Eden. Their fall in the Garden began the slide to forsaking their first love.

In 2018, I rode a bicycle across the United States from Astoria, Oregon to Yorktown, Virginia—4,320 miles of pedaling and camping along the way. Having lost my home in a fire five years prior, it was a healing journey for me. Largely a solo ride, my riding partner for a part of it became critical of me when I would order a drinking straw as we stopped for dinner, saying I would be responsible for killing whales. When we picked up groceries, she spurned all plastic bags. What a startling introduction to *eco-activism!*

I've thought much about it since then and have drawn some conclusions. One of those is that many have taken the charge to steward our earth to an unhealthy degree.

Not that we shouldn't care for what we've been provided: God commanded us to do so from the very beginning. The problem is when we begin to obsess over creation to the point of forsaking our first love; we forget who the creation belongs to, and we *begin to worship the creation, not the Creator!*

Good stewardship is one thing; obsession is quite another. Webster's Dictionary defines stewardship as, "the careful and responsible management of something entrusted to one's care." I learned a little about stewardship from a friend who owns two vases:

I have two vases with special meaning to me. One is a spectacular Czech cut crystal artisan item my husband and I purchased on a trip to Prague at a time when we had just lost everything we owned in a wildfire. It was my first beautiful purchase to begin rebuilding, and I treasure it for the memory.

But, I have another vase I treasure infinitely more. It's clay. It's a subtle beige with an abstract brown and blue "dripped" glaze strip around its center. It's also lovely, but, to anyone but me, it would not compare with the gorgeous high-end crystal from Prague!

I value the two items differently than you might expect. Why? My crystal vase is brought out only a couple of times a year to hold the occasional rose, and it adds a special touch of class to our home on such occasions. The beige clay vase proudly adorns my office, holding an arrangement of dried flowers and seed pods. It was lovingly crafted for my delight by my father. It was a gift created with *me* in mind, brought to Colorado from San Diego on one of the last trips my father made to visit us before travel became too difficult. It brings a smile to my face each morning as I walk in and am reminded that my father loves me.

Of course, any object increases in value when we personally and intimately know the maker. This same friend's daughter felt conflicted when their house burned, saying she wasn't sure what hurt more, losing their *home* or losing their *forest*. One had been built by the hands of her earthly father, the other by the hands of our Heavenly Father. Granted, many who feel deeply about any harm to the creation know the Creator intimately. In His creation, we see multi-faceted reflections of God's personality and hear a symphony of whispers of His love. Indeed, we should be thankful for God's creation and steward it well. But we must *not* allow that adoration to be replaced by obsession or idolatry.

A subset of eco-activism is called *climate change*. But it hasn't always been called that. In 1896, a seminal paper by Swedish scientist Svante Arrhenius first predicted that changes in atmospheric carbon dioxide levels could substantially alter the surface temperature through the greenhouse effect.[8] In 1938, Guy Callendar connected carbon dioxide increases in Earth's atmosphere to *global warming*.[9] *Global cooling* was a conjecture, especially during the 1970s, of imminent cooling of the Earth, culminating in a period of extensive glaciation, due to the cooling effects of aerosols.[10]

---

[8] "Evidence," *NASA Science*, https://science.nasa.gov/climate-change/evidence/.

[9] "A Brief History of Climate Change Discoveries," *UK Research and Innovation*, https://www.discover.ukri.org/a-brief-history-of-climate-change discoveries/index.html#:~:text=1938%20%2D%20Proof%20that%20 global%/';20 temperatures%20are%20rising&text=Doing%20all%20his%20 calculations%20by,were%20responsible%20for%20global%20warming.

[10] "Global Cooling," *Wikipedia*, https://en.wikipedia.org/wiki/Globa l_cooling#:~:text=Global%20cooling% 20was %20a%20conjecture, of%20 aerosols%20or%20orbital%20forcing.

Now, it's called *climate change*. My intent is neither to dwell on this nor to get into the science of it, as untold numbers of people are doing (with about as many opinions as people doing it). I would simply point out that we seem to have trouble making up our minds—is it warming, cooling, or something else? Frankly, it seems to have become more of the same—worshipping the creation and *not* the Creator.

The apostle Paul was direct about this topic as he wrote in his letter to the Romans:

> Therefore God gave them over in the sinful desires of their hearts . . . They exchanged the truth about God for a lie, and worshiped and served created things rather than the Creator—Who is forever praised. Amen.
> Romans 1:24-25

And the writer who penned Psalm 148 was equally clear in declaring the creation worships the Creator:

> Praise Him, sun and moon;
> praise Him, all you shining stars.
> Praise Him, you highest heavens

and you waters above the skies.
Let them praise the name of the LORD,
  for at His command they were created . . .
Psalm 148:3-5

We know, of course, that His creation included far more than what we see in the psalm above; it also included all the animals. It seems natural to value some animals over others—I think we all tend to do that at times. I'm reminded, though, that the original creation was perfect, with each animal filling a unique role (see Chapter 4 on evolution), and all parts were equally valuable, just as the parts of the body:

> . . . a body, though one, has many parts, but all its many parts form one body . . . Even so the body is not made up of one part but of many. . . But in fact God has placed the parts in the body, every one of them, just as He wanted them to be.
> 1 Corinthians 12:12, 14, 18

And more than that, how did some come to believe any animal is more valuable than the apex of God's creation—*man*?

> Then God said, "Let us make mankind in our image, in our likeness, so that they may rule over the fish in the sea and the birds in the sky, over the livestock and all the wild animals, and over all the creatures that move along the ground."
> Genesis 1:26

> Indeed, the very hairs of your head are all numbered. Don't be afraid; you are worth more than many sparrows.
> Luke 12:7

How easy it's become to value an animal species, particularly one that faces potential extinction, to a degree that borders on worship. Of course, there have been many instances of animal worship, called zoolatry, from the beginning of human existence; it is certainly not new. From bulls and cows to elephants and lions, and even peacocks and rats (and many more), animals have been revered as gods from time immemorial. God has spoken against zoolatry in Deuteronomy 4:15-18, where He explicitly bans the making of idols in the form of any kind of animal, bird, reptile, or fish. Most are familiar with Israel's worship of Aaron's statue of the golden calf at Mount Sinai, detailed in Exodus 32:1-35 and again in Deuteronomy 9:8-21. Again, none of this is lost on the apostle Paul, as he admonished us against worshiping and serving created things rather than the Creator (Romans 1:24-25).

Think about this for a moment: how many times have you observed people who treat their pet dogs as children, in some cases perhaps *better* than their children? Have you ever seen someone walking a pet chihuahua in a baby carriage and heard how they talk to it? It's entertaining, to say the least, but it may be that our priorities are upside down.

No doubt, it's important to protect helpless, endangered species. We were, after all, called to protect our earth and the animals God placed under our care at the beginning (see Genesis scripture cited above). But *never* should this be done at the expense of His priorities, which *always* supersede ours. He has far higher purposes than protecting animals, vis-a-vis the Great Commission, which commands us in Matthew 28:19-20 to share Him with a dying and lost world.

When we lose sight of *that* in favor of *any* other cause, it risks becoming idolatry. To illustrate the point, an op-ed appeared in the Colorado Springs Gazette in late 2023 that referred to a lawsuit filed in Colorado Springs by the Florida-based Nonhuman Rights Project on behalf of five elephants (each named) housed at the Cheyenne Mountain Zoo.[11] The plaintiff claimed a habeas corpus violation and insisted the zoo "release the animals from unlawful confinement." The 376-page lawsuit demanded the release of the elephants "to a suitable elephant sanctuary in the United States." The article went on to mention a contemporary *civil rights crusade that treats animals as equal or superior to humans* (italics mine). Fortunately (in my opinion), this lawsuit was dismissed.

But I wonder: just how many rodents, reptiles, and butterflies are the objects of such inordinate attention these days?

Consider that US Code 668-668d, enacted in 1940, prohibits "anyone, without a permit issued by the Secretary of the Interior, from taking bald or golden eagles, including their parts (even feathers), nests, or eggs. Destroying or even disturbing a bald eagle's egg or nest carries a $100,000 fine and a sentence of up to a year in prison for a first offense." Sounds like a responsible policy, doesn't it? But is it?

---

[11] "Activists Want Animals Protected as 'Persons,'" *Colorado Springs Gazette*, December 8, 2023.

We recently visited the Henry Doorly Zoo in Omaha, one of the top five in the country. Then we drove through the Wildlife Safari Park just outside of Omaha, where, in addition to some fascinating animals such as black bears, bison, and owls, they are also nursing injured bald eagles. I took this picture of a taxidermied eagle on display in the gift store and asked how they were able to own one, in light of the US Code cited above. They said they didn't own it; rather, it was on loan from the Fish and Wildlife Department. Interesting, I thought. So, I looked up the value of a stuffed bald eagle. Remarkably, according to the IRS estate tax department, it is worth $65 million. Where did this number come from, anyway? And doesn't it seem strange to place a monetary value on something that is illegal to purchase and has no known market? Makes me wonder just how one values some things these days.

According to recent data, there are over 1,300 species listed as either endangered or threatened in the United States under the Endangered Species Act.[12] Each of these can serve as a worthy cause or a distraction from what is most important. Anything can become an idol—from golden calves to possessions, to physical appearance, to addictive behaviors, to—you name it. Even animals can become objects of worship; when they do, we neglect what God holds most important for us to dwell on.

My Prayer: Father, teach me to be a good steward over Your entire creation, including the many animals You made, but *never* to worship it. *You* alone are worthy of my worship— may I always maintain a proper balance in mind, never becoming distracted from Your Great Commission to share You with others living in darkness.

---

[12] "Endangered Species: Species Information (Factsheets)," *United States Environmental Protection Agency*, May 16, 2024. https://www.epa.gov/endangered-species/endangered-species-species-information-factsheets

Should a Bank Robber be Entitled to Use the Stolen Money with Impunity?

Illegal Immigration

A masked man walked into a bank and held up a teller at gunpoint, demanding a large sum of money. The teller complied, handing him a sack of bills. He left the bank peacefully, then used the money to start an orphanage for children who'd been abused, with the hope they would grow up to be useful, productive citizens in society. The robber was eventually arrested for armed robbery and brought to trial. At his trial, he confessed to the crime but pointed out that he'd used the money for a good cause, positively impacting many lives.

The defense pointed out during cross-examination that the man was well-respected in the community and a newlywed with a toddler. Additionally, the jury dreaded the thought of the orphanage being required to pay the money back to the bank. The jury found him innocent of wrongdoing, and the judge allowed him to go free.

***

Does anyone else have a problem with this story, or is it just me? It seems that regardless of what he did with the money, his crime must be addressed. Laws mean something, and we're admonished by God to abide by the laws of the land insofar as they do not conflict with the clear teaching of

Scripture (God's higher law). If something starts badly, i.e., in lawless behavior (and I'm lumping together the breaking of both man's and God's laws here), subsequent events cannot undo, cover for, or make amends for the original act—it must be repaired at the root.

Robin Hood was *not* a good guy!

America is a country founded on laws. Laws are not just punitive; they serve to provide compassion and justice for those who have been wronged. Americans have a long history of offering compassion and seeking justice. Found on the Statue of Liberty are the following words by Emma Lazarus:

> Give me your tired, your poor, your huddled masses yearning to breathe free, the wretched refuse of your teeming shore. Send these, the homeless, tempest-tossed to me, I lift my lamp beside the golden door!

What a powerful message, which has inspired many to seek refuge in this great land! Many come here to escape oppressive regimes or otherwise horrible living conditions, but, unfortunately, in fleeing other nations' oppressive rules, they often disregard the rules of our own.

Many take jobs (often at lower wages) and do "good" things. Many attempt to integrate into society, becoming "good" citizens. But should any of that matter, as the laws of our land, and our very sovereignty, were violated at the outset? The hard fact is that what begins in lawless behavior must be dealt with at the root—the crime itself. Subsequent events or actions can't possibly reverse the lawlessness. Again, it's why we have laws, to ensure orderly conduct. It's why Jesus came to earth as fully God and fully man; He lived the life we couldn't live and died the death we all deserved. He alone provided the way for our sins to be dealt with appropriately and completely.

One of my favorite examples of this is seen in the Old Testament book of 2 Samuel 11, where the great patriarch and king David sexually sins with Bathsheba, a married woman and wife of one of David's key military figures who is on the battlefield. When David brings Uriah home from battle to cover his sin of adultery, Uriah chooses not to lie with his wife, but, instead, remains just outside the entrance to the palace until he can return to battle (he is, after all, a good soldier, faithful to his commander). Even after David gets him drunk, he still refuses to go home. David then instructs the battle commander to put Uriah out in front where the fighting is fiercest, then to withdraw from him so he will be struck down and die. When news comes back that Uriah is dead, Bathsheba mourns for her loss. After the time for mourning is over, she is brought to David where she becomes his wife and bears him a son.

Here's how the story ends: David paid a huge price for his sin—the baby died, and strife plagued his family until the end of his life. Repentance alone restored his relationship with God, who referred to him as a man after God's own heart. The sin, though, *had* to be dealt with—*first*.

Here is another more recent example that demonstrates this important truth: I was snorkeling at my favorite spot—Hanauma Bay—on the windward side of Oahu. While engaged in watching the fish along the reef, I grabbed a small black rock the size of a quarter and put it in my pocket, figuring it would make a nice souvenir from my favorite place in Hawaii. Only later did I think about the fact that taking *anything* from the Bay is unlawful, and that night I felt convicted for having done so. So much so that I took the rock back and asked the gate guard to have it returned to the beach. The misdeed *had* to be repaired at the *root*.

What's this got to do with illegal immigration? Everything—despite how oppressive the country of origin is.

I believe Emma Lazarus never intended, by her welcoming words, for our country's sovereign laws to be violated without consequence. Regardless of how open our borders may be, or how difficult it is to legally enter the country, the laws are still in place and are binding. We surely have the right to attempt to change a bad law, but, until that happens, it's *still* the law.

It was *man's* rule that I violated at Hanauma Bay; how much more concerned should I be about violating one of *God's* rules? If we believe God to be the supreme ruler of our lives, that question should be easy to answer.

> Let everyone be subject to the governing authorities, for there is no authority except that which God has established. The authorities that exist have been established by God. Consequently, whoever rebels against the authority is rebelling against what God has instituted, and those who do so will bring judgment on themselves.
> Romans 13:1-2

My prayer: Lord, may I be mindful, not only of *Your* laws but also of the laws of this land in which You've called me to peaceably live. Help me understand that subsequent events can *never* absolve what begins in sin; the sin itself must be dealt with first. Thank you, gracious God, for paying the ultimate price by dying on the cross to atone for *my* sin.

Shouldn't it Be OK to Open Christmas Presents Early if They're Carefully Rewrapped?

Sex Outside of Marriage

*I*t was a month before Christmas and six-year-old Jeremy was anxious to open one particular gift his father had wrapped in bright, shiny paper for him. He was afraid to ask permission to open it early, as his father made it clear it was *not* to be opened before Christmas morning.

Jeremy had trouble sleeping one night, tossing and turning, thinking only about the gift. He got up and sneaked down the stairs, while the rest of his family slept. He gazed for a long time at that special gift, and, in a fit of impulse, hurriedly opened it. It was beautiful to behold, *just* what he was hoping for. He played on the floor with it for a while. But he became frightened his father would find out, so he *carefully* (remember, he was six) rewrapped it so no one would notice.

He did the same thing several nights after that, each time rewrapping the gift. Christmas morning finally arrived and his father, who *had* noticed, chastised his son and made Jeremy give back the gift.

***

Does this sound unduly harsh? Could it be that we've become cold to the importance of abiding by our Heavenly Father's commands concerning the right way to live? Could *we* be the ones who've changed, while He never changes? I, for one, still believe "Jesus Christ is the same yesterday and today and forever. Do not be carried away by all kinds of strange teachings" (Hebrews 13:8-9a).

Just as He remains the same, His expectations of us have remained the same as well. It should come as no surprise that God has, at times, refused to fully bless those who've walked in rebellion against His commands—like the boy's father did in the story above. An older woman from my church related a similar story from her childhood. After she intentionally opened a gift well before Christmas, she opened it for real on Christmas morning. Her response was interesting—she *hated* it. There was no surprise; her Christmas was ruined, nothing to look forward to. It was her worst Christmas ever!

If these stories seem far-fetched, consider the biblical account of Tamar, the beautiful sister of Absalom, son of David. Tamar's half-brother Amnon fell in love with her and devised a plan to rape her despite her pleading with him not to do so. "Don't, my brother!" she said to him. "Don't force me. Such a thing should not be done in Israel! Don't do this wicked thing. What about me? Where could I get rid of my disgrace? And what about you? You would be like one of the wicked fools in Israel. Please speak to the king [David]; he will not keep me from being married to you." But he refused to listen to her, and since he was stronger than she, he raped her. Then Amnon hated her with intense hatred. In fact, he hated her more than he had loved her (2 Samuel 13:12-15).

He then sent her away in shame, and he was later murdered by his brother Absalom.[13]

As we prepare to dive into the main topic of this chapter—sex outside of marriage—allow me to ask a frank question: Might we have become culturally soft on *consensual sexual intercourse between two persons not married to each other*? Of course, the story of Tamar does not involve consensual sex, as she was raped, but the message of this chapter can be seen in each of these stories. I find it interesting that the italicized portion of the second sentence of this paragraph is Merriam Webster's word-for-word definition of *fornication*. This is important, as it is among the sinful behaviors named in Scripture that cannot be found in the Kingdom of God:

> Or do you not know that the unrighteous will not inherit the kingdom of God? Do not be deceived; neither *fornicators*, nor idolaters, nor adulterers, nor effeminate, nor homosexuals, nor thieves, nor the covetous, nor drunkards, nor revilers, nor swindlers, will inherit the kingdom of God. Such were some of you; but you were washed, but you were sanctified, but you were justified in the name of the Lord Jesus Christ and in the Spirit of our God.
> 1 Corinthians 6:9-11, NASB

> And He was saying, "That which proceeds out of the man, that is what defiles the man. For from within, out of the heart of men, proceed the evil thoughts, *fornications*, thefts, murders, adulteries, deeds of coveting and wickedness, as well as deceit, sensuality, envy, slander, pride and foolishness. All these evil things proceed from within and defile the man."
> Mark 7:20-23, NASB

---

[13] You can read the whole story in 2 Samuel 13.

And the Scriptures lay out very specific conditions for sexual intimacy:

> Now for the matters you wrote about: "It is good for a man not to have sexual relations with a woman." But since sexual immorality is occurring, each man should have sexual relations with his own wife, and each woman with her own husband . . . Now to the unmarried and the widows I say: It is good for them to stay unmarried, as I do. But if they cannot control themselves, they should marry, for it is better to marry than to burn with passion.
> 1 Corinthians 7:1-2, 8-9

> Let marriage be held in honor among all, and let the marriage bed be undefiled, for God will judge the sexually immoral and adulterous.
> Hebrews 13:4

> That is why a man leaves his father and mother and is united to his wife, and they become one flesh.
> Genesis 2:24

The clear implication of these and other Scripture verses is that God's intent was for sexual intimacy to be reserved for marriage between a man and a woman. *Period.* This expectation was certainly not lost on those alive during Jesus' time on earth. Think of what was going on in Joseph's head during his engagement to Mary when she was found pregnant by the Holy Spirit. Even Joseph had a problem with her integrity until a supernatural visitor showed up and convinced him all was above board.

Why, then, has it become popular of late to live together as a married couple would *before* marriage? Some might argue it's a smart move to ensure compatibility before a life-long commitment, sort of a try-before-you-buy scenario. But what do the facts reveal? Does that sort of test period prove effective?

An article in the *Journal of Family Issues* entitled "Re-Examining the Link Between Premarital Sex and Divorce" reveals the startling conclusion that premarital sex is linked to *higher* rates of divorce, not lower, as the try-before-you-buy scenario would promise. "It's true that premarital sex is linked to higher rates of divorce, particularly when it involves partners other than one's eventual spouse, but the nature of this relationship is poorly understood."[14] That being said, the article also points out that premarital sex with only the eventual marriage partner *also* results in a higher percentage of divorce than for those remaining chaste before marrying.

Not long ago, a pastor friend of mine recounted a conversation he had with his son about marriage and the beauty of sex that is part of a God-ordained marriage—his son was about to embark on a most serious venture: to move in with a beautiful young lady, unmarried, which was against their training and biblical teaching. He encouraged his son, saying,

> "If you choose this path, premaritally, you are establishing a rocky foundation to build upon. Whatever you build on top of this shaky foundation won't matter. I'm afraid it will collapse and crumble. Oh, we don't want that for you. Father God does not want that for you. The reason you are living in God's favor is due to the covenant that your mom and I made to be sexually pure before marriage. We are far from perfect; however, God's covenant remains strong to this very moment. We desire this for you."

---

[14] Jesse Smith and Nicholas H. Wolfinger, "Re-Examining the Link Between Premarital Sex and Divorce," *Journal of Family Issues*, February 12, 2023.

Then my friend shared the outcome, saying,

"Our son did not wait. After four years of trying to add good things on top of a faulty foundation, their marriage ended with a divorce, the opposite of a covenant. Father God is gracious, and He altogether forgives without condemning. Yet, scars remain to this day."

Do I include this story to suggest marriages beginning in sin are doomed to fail? By no means, just as marriages beginning in accordance with God's mandates are not guaranteed to succeed. It's just that when we start building a relationship in sinful behavior, atop the wrong foundation, it simply becomes more difficult to get back on track. Here's the good news—our God offers redemption and forgiveness for our failures to walk in His way. There's always hope.

The *Journal of Family Issues* article cited above further points out that while premarital sex predicts divorce, no one really knows why. Let me offer what I feel to be a pretty good, educated guess. God created the marriage institution between a man and a woman—for *life*, as we read in the Bible's first book, Genesis:

Then the Lord God said, "It is not good for the man to be alone; I will make him a helper suitable for him." And out of the ground the Lord God formed every animal of the field and every bird of the sky, and brought them to the man to see what he would call them; and whatever the man called a living creature, that was its name. The man gave names to all the livestock, and to the birds of the sky, and to every animal of the field, but for Adam there was not found a helper suitable for him. So the Lord God caused a deep sleep to fall upon the man, and he slept; then He took one of his ribs and closed up the flesh at that place. And the Lord God fashioned into a woman the rib which He had taken from the man, and brought her to the man. Then the man said,

"**At last** this is bone of my bones,
And flesh of my flesh;
She shall be called 'woman,'
Because she was taken out of man."
Genesis 2:18-23 (NASB)

I've bolded the first words of Adam when he first beheld his wife, "**At last,**" expressing great joy as he witnessed God's magnificent creation. On a lighter side, I've heard it suggested that he exclaimed, "Whoa, man!" [woman], in addition.

Marriage is a serious construct, one not to be taken lightly. Such involves (requires) serious commitment, before God and man. And that's how it was in the beginning. In fact, in Old Testament times, the bride and groom might not have ever seen each other before their marriage day. The commitment was no less real, however, and trumped all other commitments, except the commitment to follow after God. That was how I viewed the sanctity of marriage when I was very young—my parents modeled that in what turned out to be a sixty-five-year marriage relationship. And my prayer partner, Rich, mentioned to me that when he got married, his attitude was, "Holy moly, the only way out of this is death!"

So, what has changed to convince us God doesn't feel that way anymore? Why would an experimental trial period for pending marriage be considered acceptable now, especially in light of the facts regarding premarital sex and divorce? Have God's rules become less important today? Here's a question that bears great weight on this topic: Why would a man *want* to spend a lifetime with a woman who says *no* to sex before marriage? The only answer I can think of is that he truly loves her, trusts her, and is committed to her.

Tim Keller, in his book *The Meaning of Marriage*,[15] speaks of two types of marriage: a commercial one, which is conditional (and one that seems to be pervading our culture), and a covenant one, which is *all in*, truly for better or worse. My thought is that we, as a culture, have bought into the first and disdained the latter. We would be well-advised to remember God's idea of marriage from the very beginning represented a covenant relationship that modeled His special commitment to His people. It's a parallel picture of Christ and His Church, a sacred relationship—for *life*. That's the foundation upon which our married lives should be built. The pure gift of sex is most special when it's used as intended—in marriage between a man and a woman.

As I conclude this chapter, let's hearken to my pastor friend's story and how he now reflects on it. "As I shared, regarding my son who chose not to wait to build a sacred relationship with his wife, he learned an eternal lesson, which I share with you. As we find in Ecclesiastes 3:11, *He* (God Himself) *has put eternity in their (our) hearts*. It's already done! My son now views relationships through this lens—a lens of eternity—not just a bigger picture, but the biggest picture!"

We would all be served well if we were willing, as soon as possible, to heed the words of King David: "I have hidden your word in my heart that I might not sin against you" (Psalm 119:11).

My Prayer: Dear Lord, may we not lose sight of your mandates, designed to protect us, never to harm us. Help us remember that You have not changed—we have. May we

---

[15] Tim Keller, *The Meaning of Marriage*, (Penguin Group, 2011).

fall in love once more with the eternal God who loved us first. Burn into our hearts the desire to please You above all else. May we think not only about today, this moment, but view things from Your eternal perspective. After all, You've placed eternity in our hearts—*may we live it!* Convince us as a nation of the importance of returning to our roots in You.

Aren't There Many Ways That Jigsaw Puzzle Pieces Can Fit Together?

Homosexuality

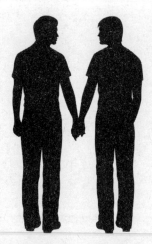

*T*welve-year-old Jenny was working on a jigsaw puzzle—one of her favorite activities at home. Somewhere in the middle, she found two pieces that didn't fit perfectly, but she decided to leave them that way because she liked the way they looked together. Her father said, "Honey, I don't think those two go together," but she insisted they did and pressed on with the project.

As she approached the finish, she noticed she was missing a piece but did not consider it might be one of the two she had put together earlier. Her father suggested splitting them up to see if one of them was the missing piece, but she was determined they belonged together and left them where they were. The puzzle remained unfinished.

***

Jenny's fundamental problem was her failure to recognize the jigsaw designer's decision to create a puzzle that could be correctly completed *only* one way. Close was simply not close enough. Any configuration other than the intended one couldn't work—ever. It's the same with Sudoku, wooden puzzle cubes, or you name it; only one configuration works properly, the one the designer intended.

What's this got to do with the emotionally charged topic of homosexuality? What's wrong with two men (or two women) falling in love and living happily together as a married couple might, so long as they don't bother anyone else? They love each other, after all. That may seem like a logical question to ask. But is it? By that same logic, would it be OK for a forty-year-old man to fall in love and cohabit with his fourteen-year-old niece, as a married couple would? Most would immediately answer no without even thinking about it. How about a seventeen-year-old teenage boy having sexual relations with his female collie, whom he loves very much? Same answer I suspect. But we really should ask the question, what makes these situations so different? Some might suggest a fourteen-year-old girl is incapable of making such a decision that involves falling in love with an adult partner. She's too young, they believe. And the boy with the dog? Well, that's just wrong! *Who* says? Is it the same people who say it's OK for two adult males to do so? Doesn't that appear rather arbitrary?

Let's look at some documented, natural consequences of homosexual behaviors. Many factors can increase or decrease HIV risk among youth. The Centers for Disease Control and Prevention's (CDC) "National Youth Risk Behavior Survey" and other CDC data have identified five leading risk factors that can increase adolescents' and young adults' risk of *Human Immunodeficiency Virus* (HIV); the one that struck me as most interesting was **male-male sex.** Young men who have sex with men, especially those who are Black/African American and Hispanic/Latino, have high rates of new HIV diagnoses. *Anal* sex is the riskiest type of sex for getting or transmitting HIV (italics mine).[16]

Doesn't this tell us something? Could it be that men were not designed to have sex with men? And the same for women with women? As crude as this may sound, does it make any logical sense that an exit orifice should be used as an *entrance*?

In an interesting article, Robert L Kinney III wrote, "homosexually inclined people have been shown to be at higher risk of major depression, anxiety, and suicidality than heterosexuals."[17] He further pointed out that in the 1980s and early 1990s, the outbreak of HIV and Acquired Immunodeficiency Syndrome (AIDS) swept pandemically across the United States and the rest of the world, though the disease originated decades earlier. At the time of this writing, more than 70 million people had been infected with HIV and about 35 million had died from AIDS since the start of the pandemic, according to the World Health Organization (WHO). Updated figures are reflected in a 2023 article by the Global Health Observatory: Since the beginning of the epidemic, 88.4 million [71.3–112.8 million] people have been infected with HIV, and about 42.3 million [35.7–51.1 million] people have died of HIV. Globally, 39.9 million [36.1–44.6 million] people were living with HIV at the end of 2023.[18]

As in all the other chapters contained in this book, if we were not created by a higher power, then we can serve as our own higher power and thus create our own rules. However, if

---

[16] Youth Risk and Behavior Survey: Data Summary and Trends Report, Centers for Disease Control and Prevention, 2023, https://www.cdc.gov/healthyyouth/data/yrbs/pdf/yrbs_data-summary-trends_report2023_508.pdf.

[17] R.L. Kinney III, "Homosexuality and Scientific Evidence: On Suspect Anecdotes, Antiquated Data, and Broad Generalizations," *NIH National Library of Medicine*, 2015, https://pubmed.ncbi.nlm.nih.gov/26997677/.

[18] https://www.who.int/data/gho/data/themes/hivaids#:~:text=Global%20situation%20and%20trends%3A,at%20the %20end%20of%202023.

we truly *are* created beings, then we are accountable to a Holy God who knows what's best for us. It's really that simple. God is not at all silent on these issues, and our belief in what He says matters:

> Therefore God gave them up in the lusts of their hearts to impurity, to the dishonoring of their bodies among themselves, because they exchanged the truth about God for a lie and worshiped and served the creature rather than the Creator, who is blessed forever! Amen. For this reason God gave them up to dishonorable passions. For their women exchanged natural relations for those that are contrary to nature; and the men likewise gave up natural relations with women and were consumed with passion for one another, men committing shameless acts with men and receiving in themselves the due penalty for their error.
> Romans 1:24-27, ESV

> You shall not lie with a male as with a woman; it is an abomination.
> Leviticus 18:22, ESV

Solomon noted in Ecclesiastes that there is nothing new under the sun. Thus, it shouldn't surprise anyone that homosexual behavior is not new either. We read in Genesis 19:1-19 how Lot admitted two angels into the protection of his home when, before they had gone to bed, all the men from every part of the city of Sodom—both young and old— surrounded the house. They called to Lot, "Where are the men who came to you tonight? Bring them out to us so that we can have sex with them" (vs. 4-5). The end was total devastation for the city, as God rained down burning sulfur on it in judgment, as can be seen in the remainder of the passage.

In the late 1980s, our church in Burlington, Massachusetts, hosted a famous Christian singer-songwriter. This man wrote and sang music that I loved listening to. I knew his music well; what I didn't know, and was surprised to find out, was that he struggled with homosexuality most of his life. Some years before his visit he had a supernatural encounter with the living God, who convinced him homosexuality displeased his Creator. He related how he had to allow God to remove the foundational beliefs he had spent his lifetime building upon, and then replace them with proper life principles that could only come from his Maker.

Here's the most amazing part of this story: He shared how he got married and fathered nine children. While he, at times, felt a bit odd about being married to a *woman* and becoming a father, he knew he was living in God's will and was becoming more and more joyful at fulfilling exactly who God called him to be.

The good news here is that homosexuals are not without hope—Jesus came to make all things new, especially our hearts. God is for us. His heart is for us. His hopes and dreams are for us. He longs for us to come to him so He can fulfill His promise:

"... For I know the plans I have for you, declares the Lord, "plans to prosper you and not to harm you, plans to give you hope and a future."
Jeremiah 29:11

My Prayer: Lord, may I learn to respect that *You* are God, and I am not. You have sound reasons for the natural order that You've laid out for us as Your dearly loved children. Help us appreciate Your sound reasons for creating some to be male and some to be female. May we seek the best You have offered to us and never settle for less.

Don't You Understand that What's Yours is Mine?

Entitlement Mentality

*J*ames joined his third-grade classmates as they walked into the cafeteria for lunch. But instead of getting into the buffet line to select what he wanted, he went to a table and sat down. His classmates joined him at the table and began to eat.

One of them asked, "Aren't you going to eat?"

James replied, "Sure I am, but I'm not about to wait in line; someone should bring me my meal."

When his classmates were finishing up, a cafeteria staff member noticed he hadn't eaten and asked him if he wanted lunch.

"Well, duh!"

The staff member went back to the kitchen, prepared him a lunch, and delivered it to him—without so much as a thank you.

***

This story never would have happened when I was growing up, but, unfortunately, hints at how we've changed as a culture. I was taught that if I studied hard in school, went to college, and persevered, then I would land a good job, be able to pay my bills, and even have enough to buy some things I wanted. This was the land of opportunity, to be sure, and there was no limit to what someone could achieve—the operative word being *achieve*. Entitlement mentality, in contrast, says it is the land of free handouts.

While entitlement mentality typically has little to do with school buffet lines, it certainly is something we've moved into as a culture; it's not only widespread, but it's growing. And it leads to the belief that one cannot do anything for himself/herself. A recent op-ed piece by Cal Thomas sums it up well, "The answer is that so many people have been misled to rely on government first and themselves last that they have become addicted to government and the borrowed money that keeps those checks coming."[19]

It didn't start here, however. We see an excellent example of entitlement mentality in the Old Testament. There, Naaman was commander of the army of the king of Aram. Though he was great and highly regarded by the king, he had leprosy. A young Israeli girl urged him to visit the prophet Elisha in Samaria who she said would be able to cure him of his disease. Elisha told him to wash himself in the Jordan River seven times, and his flesh would be restored as evidence of his healing.

What an offer! "But Naaman went away angry and indignant, exclaiming, 'I thought that he would surely come out to me and stand and call on the name of the Lord his God, wave his hand over the spot and cure me of my leprosy'" (2 Kings 5:11). Naaman felt it demeaning for a man of his high position to do something as low as Elisha suggested. He felt entitled. Only when he complied with the prophet's suggestion, however, was he healed—physically *and* spiritually.[20] We see other Bible characters are not immune to this same mentality, e.g., Jonah, Balaam, and David, to name a few.

Why has entitlement mentality taken such hold in the United States? Whatever the reason, we see it manifesting in many new areas. This is not to imply any of these are bad,

---

[19] Cal Thomas, "President and Congress Need an Intervention," *Colorado Springs Gazette*, March 13, 2024.
[20] You can read more of this story in 2 Kings 5.

without any redeeming value, only that the way they're managed leads to more of the same —entitlement mentality.

Minimum Wage

Probably the most important aspect of America's economic system, and what distinguishes it from any other, is that of the *free* market. Any time the government imposes artificial regulations on the economy it becomes less free. This is seen in a required minimum wage—something I've always viewed as an impediment to a free economy; it seems to me that, in a free market, the business owner should have the right to pay whatever wage he/she wishes. The prospective employee then has the right to accept the offer, negotiate a higher wage, or decline the offer and look for work elsewhere.

Any attempt by the government to dictate a required minimum wage only causes problems for the employer *and* the employee. Employees are quick to remind the employer that he/she needs to pay them more now, but it's not very long before the employees ask for raises, as the cost of living has gone up. A vicious cycle ensues, driving everything up, i.e., rising minimum wages drive prices, which, in turn, drive minimum wages. Why should this sequence surprise anyone?

Did Nobel economics prize winner Milton Friedman, an American economist and statistician, see the handwriting on the wall half a century ago when he stated during a 1973 interview, "I've often said the minimum-wage rate is the most anti-negro law on the books?"[21] How about a March 24, 2024, Associated Press article stating that Lyft and Uber intend to halt operations in Minneapolis because of a city ordinance to

---

[21] Milton Friedman, Goodreads, https://www.goodreads.com/quotes/726 0512-we-regard-the-minimum-wage-rate-as-one-of-the#:~:text =Sign%20Up%20Now-We%20regard%20the%20minimum%20wage% 20rate%20as%20one%20of%20the,them%20to%20get%20good%20 wages.

increase wages for app-based drivers? This decision came on the heels of the city's council vote "to override a mayoral veto and require that ride-hailing services increase driver wages to the equivalent of the local minimum wage of $15.57 an hour."[22]

Another example is from a recent op-ed piece by Larry Elder, bestselling author and nationally syndicated radio talk-show host. On April 5, 2024, the new California $20-per-hour minimum wage for fast-food workers (25% higher than the prevailing minimum wage) has already impacted restaurant owners who've announced they are forced to shut down operations. California Pizza Hut franchisees promptly let go more than 1,200 delivery workers. Rubio's Coastal Grill, a fish taco chain, just as quickly closed all forty-eight state locations, saying, "The closings were brought about by the rising cost of doing business in California." It should come as no surprise that Wendy's concurrently increased its prices 8%, Chipotle 7.5%, and Starbucks 7%. Elder then adds that things could have been worse—Democrat US Senate candidate Barbara Lee advocates a $50 per hour minimum wage.[23]

Where does it all end? That's a good question.

Welfare and Unemployment—Two Sides of the Same Coin

On its surface, welfare sounds like a philanthropic endeavor, helping those who just can't find jobs to pay their bills. Presumably, they are all trying to find better jobs, and, thus, get off welfare. But does it really work that way? While welfare recipients are required to seek work, many simply do not do so earnestly, except to meet the requirements by applying but

---

[22] Tricia Ahmed, "Here's what we Know about Uber and Lyft's Planned Exit from Minneapolis in May," *Associated Press*, https://apnews.com/article/lyft-uber-minneapolis-ridehailing-apps-66d2f56486557733b355 39ecd97275a7.

[23] Larry Elder, "California: Where the Circus is Always in Town," *Colorado Springs Gazette*, June 7, 2024.

not really wanting to work. The program actually encourages many to remain in the same position, living in a continuous state of entitlement mentality.

Much like welfare, unemployment provides a way for many to enjoy free benefits without truly seeking employment. Many recipients of unemployment have become good at meeting the quota of jobs applied for without earnestly wanting to get one. I witnessed this firsthand as the owner of a family-practice optometry clinic for twenty years.

Employee Medical Leave, Family Medical Leave, COVID Leave, Medical Insurance, etc.

These programs sound great for employees and their families, and, when proposed by the employer, can be wonderful, uplifting benefits. Indeed, they can serve as long-term employee retention tools. But, when mandated by the government, be it Federal, State, or City, these can be devastating to employers, especially small business employers, *and* their employees.

One of our favorite Mexican restaurants, Jose Muldoon's on the northeast part of Colorado Springs, announced that it closed in early 2024 after successfully operating for thirteen years. Here are the reasons cited by the owner for having to close this popular restaurant: "An increase in Colorado's minimum wage, inflation, government mandates such as the state's new Family and Medical Leave Insurance Program that's funded through employer and employee payroll taxes, and higher property taxes and insurance costs all contributed to financial hurdles for the northeast Jose's."[24] In short, these requirements were too costly for them to remain in business.

---

[24] Rich Laden, "Northeast Jose' Muldoon's Closes: Original Property Downtown Will Remain Open, Celebrate 50th Anniversary This Year," *Gazette Telegraph*, January 19, 2024.

This news, and other news like it, should surprise no one. It saddens me as I observe the seeming destruction of the magnificent economy that *was* the United States. And what all this leads to is an entitlement mentality, which turns normal desires into expectations, the extent of which I've not seen before. How about a couple more current examples?

Student Loan Debt Forgiveness

An August 16, 2023, op-ed piece by Brett Wilkins, entitled, "62% of Student Loan Borrowers Say They're Likely to Boycott Repayments," cites the following reasons from borrowers inclined to boycott loan repayments:

- "I simply do not have the money."
- "We have not been paying for so long, so why not just do away with the student loans?"
- "Because I think some of the loans are predatory and unfair."[25]

And support for this sort of thinking is increasing, despite a legally binding contract signed by each borrower. Clearly, a legal responsibility has somehow become an entitlement expectation.

Shoplifting

You may have noticed a spike in shoplifting at stores. Self-checkouts are vanishing due to the ease of abuse. Store management has built shoplifting into its business expectations, believing nothing can be done about it. Xavier Suggs, a freshman sociology major at Hofstra, sums up all-

---

[25] Brett Wilkins, "62% of Student Loan Borrowers Say They're Likely to Boycott Repayments: Poll," *Creative Commons*, August 16, 2023.

too-common thinking in the *Hofstra Chronicle:*

> "... not all shoplifting is created equal. The right and wrong of shoplifting doesn't come from *what* you're stealing or *how much* you're stealing but *who* (sic) you're stealing from. You shouldn't be shoplifting from your local markets and small businesses that are just trying to make a living. But the mega-franchises and superstores are fair game. These companies don't care about you, only your pockets, so why should you care about their profit margins?" (Italicized emphases mine)[26]

Am I the only one bothered by this expressed attitude?

The Bible is clear that we, as God's children, are obligated to work for what we receive: "For even when we were with you, we gave you this rule: 'The one who is unwilling to work shall not eat'" (2 Thessalonians 3:10). This clear mandate does *not*, however, discount the importance of charity in meeting the needs of the poor. In fact, that's precisely how the early church helped the needy. It's important that we do that but from our desire to serve Him, *not* due to a government-mandated program.

As a positive, successful example of this kind of support, our campus of a multi-location church operates a food pantry and collects food, enabling it to provide food to ten Title 1 schools, packing and delivering to the schools 500 bags per month. The bags include individual items for breakfast, lunch, and a snack. In addition, each bag has items that can be used for the entire family to help lighten the grocery load, such as bags of rice and boxes of cereal, pasta, and pasta sauce. The schools identify their families in need and give us

---

[26] Xavier Suggs, "Shoplifting Isn't Necessarily Wrong," Hofstra Chronicle, September 27, 2023, https://www.thehofstrachronicle.com/category/editorials/2023/9/27/shoplifting-isnt-necessarily-wrong.

a number for the bags they need. We don't vet or decide who gets what—the school counselor or liaison does.

The district we're in saw three more schools designated Title 1 this school year, meaning at least 45% of their population is below a certain income level. When we consider all four campuses of our church, we provide roughly 1,000 food bags monthly, which takes care of all schools, the senior ministry, and families that connect with our assistance through Family Life Services.

Our church is not special because we do this; we do this because our relationship with Christ is special and encourages us to seek His heart by following His word:

> In everything I did, I showed you that by this kind of hard work we must help the weak, remembering the words the Lord Jesus himself said: "It is more blessed to give than to receive.
> Acts 20:35

> If anyone has material possessions and sees a brother or sister in need but has no pity on them, how can the love of God be in that person? Dear children, let us not love with words or speech but with actions and in truth.
> 1 John 3:17-18

My Prayer: Lord, please search my heart to see if there is any sign of the spirit of entitlement. Pluck it out, if there is, and replace it with the heart of Jesus in serving those less fortunate than I. May I become one who helps those caught up in the spirit of entitlement mentality to become more aware of *Your* call on their lives. Stir *Your* church to action!

The Bottom Line: A Wake-Up Call to the Church

A pastor spoke the following from the pulpit:

> "A good-looking young couple recently approached me at an altar asking for a word of blessing regarding their relationship. Expecting me to just quickly bless them, they bowed their heads immediately. Without even seeking the Lord, I said, 'Are you two sleeping together?' The look on their faces as their heads snapped up was priceless. They didn't even have to answer me. I said, 'You are asking me to bless something that the Word of God has clearly called sinful. You don't need a word of blessing. What you need to do is repent of your sins, stop sleeping together, separate, and then I'll pray God's blessing upon you.' They marched out of that church faster than I could blink and gave me the middle finger on the way out the door."

***

This story elicits, in a nutshell, what I believe to be paramount as I wrap up this book of articles that are designed to effectively (and sensitively) confront the cultural lies of the enemy. We're all familiar with these lies; we see them every day, as we are bombarded with them from all sides. I wonder if we Christians are becoming numb to them and, perhaps, even persuaded to believe them to be compatible with historic Christian theology. As I mentioned in the introduction, it appears as though wokeism, defined as a growing awareness of racial prejudice/discrimination, social justice, LGBTQ+, sexism (prejudice based on gender), and other like-issues, is putting us all to sleep. That's why I intentionally inserted a common thread question into each piece, that being, "Who is God to you? Is it the One who created the universe and everything in it, *including you*, who thus has the sovereign right to decide everything He chooses to, or—is it *you*?" If we cannot convey the relevance of the answer to this critical question to those caught up in these lies, then any attempts at persuasion become much more difficult, if not impossible.

I readily confess that when I first heard the story above, I thought, "Wow, how bold and nervy of that pastor—that's just rude! I certainly wouldn't have approached the couple in that manner." Be honest—how did *you* feel about it? But how much of the story do we really know? Is it possible he knew them well, including their story? Regardless of the pastor's approach to the young couple, however, my being taken aback made me wonder if I might be buckling to societal pressure to compromise with the clear teaching of Scripture. After having a chance to think and pray about it, I've become far less critical of his action and more awakened to the message; in fact, I think this story has much to teach the church. You see, the church *is* falling asleep, in my view— not every group of believers, to be sure, but far too many to ignore. Consider how, in 2020, the Pew Research Center published the results of a research project showing 57% of professing Christians say sex between unmarried couples in a committed relationship is sometimes or always acceptable.[27] Where did this come from, considering the biblical teaching that marriage between one man and one woman is the only God-sanctioned construct for sex found in the Scriptures? Consider just one of many examples:

---

[27] Jeff Diamant, "Half of U.S. Christians Say Casual Sex Between Consenting Adults is Sometimes or Always Acceptable," *Pew Research Center*, https://www.pewresearch.org/short-reads/2020/08/31/half-of-u-s-christians-say-casual-sex-between-consenting-adults-is-sometimes-or-always-acceptable/#:~:text=A%20majority%20of%20Christians%20(57,and%2046%25%20of%20evangelical%20Protestants.

> Marriage is to be held in honor among all, and the
> marriage bed is to be undefiled; for fornicators and
> adulterers God will judge.
> Hebrews 13:4

Many of our church leaders/pastors are failing their Lord and us. If we are inconsistent in our teaching of His Word and allow ourselves to believe it doesn't mean what it says, why should anyone believe us, or the truth? And if we are being misled by our church leaders in their failure to: (a) provide spiritual guidance, (b) teach the Word of God, and (c) equip believers for ministry (the very hallmark duties of their charge as pastor), what should we expect?

> For it is time for judgment to begin with God's
> household; and if it begins with us, what will the
> outcome be for those who do not obey the gospel
> of God?
> 1 Peter 4:17

> Not many of you should become teachers, my fellow
> believers, because you know that we who teach will
> be judged more strictly.
> James 3:1

A few recent events are not only alarming but should wake us up; these and others pose significant risks to the church's effectiveness in meeting its Great Commission mandate found at the very end of the Gospel of Matthew. Let us look at a recent ruling from the Vatican, a teaching from a prominent evangelical pastor, and the Methodist church's current opinion on pastors. These represent but a small subset of examples I might draw from, but they should serve to drive the point home.

The Vatican

The Vatican has ruled that priests may offer a blessing over same-sex couples, lending much confusion over its stand on homosexuality, despite its "clarification" that imparting blessings to same-sex couples was "not a justification of all their actions, and they are not an endorsement of the life that they lead." Further, the ruling should not be considered "heretical, contrary to the tradition of the church or blasphemous."[28] The document explains a radical change in Vatican policy by insisting people seeking God's love and mercy shouldn't be subject to "an exhaustive moral analysis" to receive it. Additionally, Pope Francis says homosexuality is a sin but not a crime. And the blessing, per Francis, should not be offered in countries that outlaw homosexuality. Hmm, I thought sin was a crime against God. Are you confused? I am, and I feel as though this position is nothing more than a political one.

An Evangelical Pastor

The renowned evangelical preacher Andy Stanley (son of the late Charles Stanley) has suggested in an October 1, 2023, sermon at his North Point Community Church in Atlanta that gay people "find themselves in a battle not against a behavior . . . but in a battle against a defining attraction that they did not choose, but somehow has chosen them." He went on to say that same-sex attraction "is not like anything that heterosexual Christians have battled. This is a category all unto itself." Further, he stated, "All of us have felt shame about things we've done. All of us have felt shame about things we haven't done. But I bet you've never carried shame about who you are. That's the difference."[29]

---

[28] Angela Giuffrida in Rome, "Vatican: Same-Sex Couples Ruling is Not Endorsement of Homosexuality," January 4, 2024.

[29] Denny Burk, "Andy Stanley's Version of Christianity," *CBMW.org*, October 1, 2023, https://cbmw.org/2023/10/01/andy-stanleys-version-christianity/.

Really? I see a problem with this, and you should, too. I watched this sermon intently over the internet, and that's precisely what he said. What I'm hearing in his message is the following:

1. "If you're homosexual, you are welcome here." I totally agree with this.
2. "If you're homosexual, God loves you exactly as you are." I totally agree with this.
3. "If you're homosexual, God doesn't expect you to change—it's who you are." *That's* where I feel Stanley, and his followers, have a major issue.

After all, God is in the *business* of conforming His children into the likeness of Christ: "Therefore, if anyone is in Christ, he is a new creation; the old has gone, the new has come!" (2 Corinthians 5:17).

In fairness to Stanley, he touts his September 28-29 *Unconditional* conference (just before the October 1 sermon) as "pastoral" in nature, designed to empower parents to better interact with their LGBTQ children, while restoring family relationships. He goes on to state that his church still teaches biblical marriage is the union of one man and one woman and sex outside of that construct is not God's best. Sounds good until he goes on to say the two featured conference speakers, both in gay marriages, are also "Christ-followers today" though they reject biblical teaching on marriage/sexuality. Stanley adds, "The men and women I know who are gay, their faith and their confidence in God dwarfs mine."[30] This seems to imply that merely professing to adhere to the biblical definition of marriage absolves one of any responsibility for a lifestyle of rebellion against clear biblical

---

[30] Ibid

mandates. It looks like not only a lack of regard for the Word of God, but a slick form of sending mixed messages.

Yes, we come to Christ *just* as we are, but that doesn't mean we *stay* just as we are. So, can one be both a homosexual and a Christian? Here's my answer: Yes and no. Am I being wishy-washy? I think not. To paraphrase John Lynch who stated in his book *The Cure,* "God is the only one who can honestly say, 'I love you just the way you are, and now I want to change you.'"[31] Another way I've seen that same sentiment presented is, "I love you as you are, but I love you too much to let you stay there." We must remember that *struggling* with a particular sin does *not* mean we are condemned, encouraged, or expected to remain in that condition—God intends to change us and our desires. We must remember that struggling with sin simply validates how we are born with a sinful nature—it does not mean it is an identity we are destined to live with. My determination that God made me a certain way—you name it—is simply not true and denies the very sin nature/flesh we've all shared since the time of Adam.

The Bible's account of the woman caught in adultery is illustrative:

> . . . but Jesus went to the Mount of Olives.
>
> At dawn He appeared again in the temple courts, where all the people gathered around Him, and He sat down to teach them. The teachers of the law and the Pharisees brought in a woman caught in adultery. They made her stand before the group and said to Jesus, "Teacher, this woman was caught in the act of adultery. In the Law Moses commanded us to stone such women. Now what do You say?" They

---

[31] John Lynch, *The Cure,* (CrossSection Publishing, San Clemente, CA, 2011).

were using this question as a trap, in order to have a basis for accusing Him.

But Jesus bent down and started to write on the ground with His finger. When they kept on questioning Him, He straightened up and said to them, "Let any one of you who is without sin be the first to throw a stone at her." Again He stooped down and wrote on the ground.

At this, those who heard began to go away one at a time, the older ones first, until only Jesus was left, with the woman still standing there. Jesus straightened up and asked her, "Woman, where are they? Has no one condemned you?" "No one, sir," she said. "Then neither do I condemn you," Jesus declared. **"Go now and leave your life of sin."**
John 8:1-11 (emphasis added)

Note that Jesus declares the woman is not condemned but then quickly admonishes her to leave her life of sin—that's His methodology with His children.

As uncomfortable as it may seem to our earthly nature, we must be submissive to His transformative process, or we're just kidding ourselves. We must be *willing* to be changed into His likeness—it's really that simple. He's preparing us to live with Him for eternity, in which there is no sin. He is the one, after all, who wrote the rules, and we must believe *that*, above all else, lest we become our own god. And let's not forget He is not bashful in calling out sin, never leaving it up to His creation to do so; Paul's admonition to the Corinthians bears repeating here:

Or do you not know that the unrighteous will not inherit the kingdom of God? Do not be deceived; neither the sexually immoral, nor idolaters, nor adulterers, nor homosexuals, nor thieves, nor the

greedy, nor those habitually drunk, nor verbal abusers, nor swindlers, will inherit the kingdom of God. Such were some of you; but you were washed, but you were sanctified, but you were justified in the name of the Lord Jesus Christ and in the Spirit of our God.
1 Corinthians 6:9-11

In this respect, *God is narrow-minded and unrelenting, not* as open-minded as some would like to think. Yes, He shows His children grace, but that is never to be taken lightly.

The Methodist Church

The United Methodist Church (UMC) recently repealed its ban on LGBTQ+ clergy, removing a long-standing rule forbidding "self-avowed practicing homosexuals" from being ordained or appointed as ministers. The vote was 692 to 51, making the denomination appear truly "united," until one realizes the vote followed the departure of more than 7,600 US congregations between 2019 and 2023— one-quarter of all UMC congregations in the country. This mass departure reflects conservative dismay over the UMC's refusal to enforce its ban originally enacted in 1984, when the conference also voted to require "fidelity in marriage and celibacy in singleness."[32]

The article goes on to report that delegates also voted 523 to 161 to change the previous definition of marriage (as only between a man and a woman) and now approve the ordination of gay Methodist ministers who may perform same-sex marriages. Interestingly, they struck language that

---

[32] Peter Smith, "United Methodists Repeal Longstanding Ban on LGBTQ Clergy," *Associated Press*, May 1, 2024.

formerly called homosexual behavior "incompatible with Christian teaching," thus violating their Book of Discipline.

"It seemed like such a simple vote, but it carried so much weight and power, as *50 years of restricting the Holy Spirit's call on people's lives* has been lifted," said Bishop Karen Oliveto, the first openly lesbian bishop in the UMC (italics added), per Smith in the same article.[33] The italicized words seem confusing and beg three questions:

1. Does man have the power to restrict the Holy Spirit, as she implies?
2. Does God only call non-sinners to His service?
3. Does the fact that an organized church approves habitual sin mean God is OK with it?

We know that if God only called non-sinners, no one would be called. Think of David, Moses, and Paul—they each had great sins in their lives, but they repented and allowed God to transform them. This much we can rely on—those whom God calls *will* be changed. Is it possible that many who think they are called, actually are not?

As I close this book of (hopefully) helpful articles, may we be reminded of three especially important things: (1) biblical truth, (2) who God is, and (3) the grace of God.

Biblical Truth

We must be *grounded* in the historical truths contained in His Word, the Bible, recognizing they *never* change. We must also *stand our ground* in the midst of pressure to accept what is contrary to biblical mandates. That includes pressure from pastors and other churchgoers. We should never accept as "normal" that which is not. God alone defines what is normal.

---

[33] Ibid

Let us always be mindful of His truth.

First from Judges:

> In those days Israel had no king; everyone did as
> they saw fit.
> Judges 21:25

The great Apostle Paul warns Timothy against apostolic
teaching by writing:

> For the time will come when people will not put
> up with sound doctrine. Instead, to suit their own
> desires, they will gather around them a great number
> of teachers to say what their itching ears want to hear.
> 2 Timothy 4:3

Again, one of my favorite verses from James, but certainly
a challenging one:

> Consider it pure joy, my brothers and sisters,
> whenever you face trials of many kinds, because
> you know that the testing of your faith produces
> perseverance. Let perseverance finish its work so
> that you may be mature and complete, not lacking
> anything."
> James 1:2-4

But we are not without hope; God continually encourages
us as we strive to serve Him:

> "I can do all things through him who strengthens
> me.
> Philippians 4:13

Who God Is

At the risk of unnecessary redundancy, may we be mindful of the fundamental question permeating every one of these articles: Who is God to you?

Again, I stress that if we cannot convey the relevance of the answer to this critical question, then any attempts at persuasion become much more difficult, if not impossible. This book of articles can be useful in convincing one to use logical thinking about these contentious issues, but they cannot stand alone. We, as Christ followers, must remember our primary job is to *make disciples of all nations* (Matthew 28:19). To do so we must pray, care for those He places on our hearts, speak the truth in love, and trust Him to do the work that He alone can do.

And let us not forget what Jerry White, President Emeritus of The Navigators, International, so eloquently stated, "One cannot persuade *and* antagonize at the same time." I believe this idea cannot be summarized any better than the words of Charles Spurgeon: "The Gospel is a very *fearless gospel*, it boldly proclaims the truth, whether men like it or not: we must be equally faithful and unflinching. But the gospel is also *very gentle* . . . Let us seek to win others by the gentleness of our words and acts. It is the message of the God of love to a lost and fallen race . . . We must not forget that the gospel of Christ is holy. It never excuses sin: it pardons it, but only through an atonement."[34]

The Grace of God

As we share with those caught up in these cultural lies, we must remember no one is beyond God's reach until their last breath. There is no sin so great that He is not willing to

---

[34] C.H. Spurgeon, *Morning & Evening: Daily Readings, May 24th Evening*, (Christian Focus Publications, 1994).

forgive. He loves us far more than we love ourselves, after all, and His commandments are there *because* of that love—they're to *protect* us, never to harm us. But here's the catch—we must be willing to recognize *Him*, and not us, as God. We must be willing to agree with Him. He wants us to change our thinking and submit to His process for conforming us to His image; our part is to allow Him to do just that. Otherwise, we truly are kidding ourselves.

As we seek to share the Good News with those to whom He calls us, we must be mindful that preparation is critically important. This involves spending time *daily* with Jesus, drawing close to Him, studying His Word, praying, and putting on the armor of God. He will never fail us. We trust the Holy Spirit to guide us, and we encourage our friends and families to do the same. Earnestly seeking Him is precisely how we become equipped to convince others of who God is, and how the Bible is relevant *today*.

> Dear friends, although I was very eager to write to you about the salvation we share, I felt compelled to write and urge you to contend for the faith that was once for all entrusted to God's holy people. For certain individuals whose condemnation was written about long ago have secretly slipped in among you. They are ungodly people, who pervert the grace of our God into a license for immorality and deny Jesus Christ our only Sovereign and Lord. Jude 3-4

> Finally, be strong in the Lord and in his mighty power. Put on the full armor of God, so that you can take your stand against the devil's schemes. For our struggle is not against flesh and blood, but against the rulers, against the authorities, against the

powers of this dark world and against the spiritual forces of evil in the heavenly realms.
Ephesians 6:10-12

May God richly pour out His blessings upon you as you endeavor to fulfill His Great Commission in the truth and light of the Gospel, with the attitude of Christ, and in love.

About the Author

After a twenty-five-year Air Force career following graduation from the U.S. Air Force Academy, John Rabins fulfilled a boyhood dream of becoming an optometrist. He graduated from the New England College of Optometry in Boston, then operated a family practice clinic in Colorado Springs for twenty-two years before retiring from the profession in 2022. Residing in the beautiful Black Forest for thirty years with his wife, their dogs, cats, and snake (who, believe it or not, is over 45 years old), John enjoys spending time outdoors, particularly hiking in Colorado's mountains and riding his bike. This, his third published book, follows the multiple-award-winning *Defined by Fire: Seven Life-Changing Lessons from Devastating Tragedy,* and *Spiritual Musings from the Saddle of a Bicycle* (devotional from a 4,320-mile bike ride across the U.S. in 2018, from Astoria, Oregon to Yorktown, Virginia).